NOR
DOG FRIENDLY
PUB WALKS

ANGELA YOUNGMAN

COUNTRYSIDE BOOKS
NEWBURY BERKSHIRE

First published 2024
© 2024 Angela Youngman

All rights reserved. No part of this publication may be reproduced, stored
in a retrieval system, or transmitted by any means, electronic, mechanical,
photocopying, recording or otherwise, without the prior written
permission of the copyright holder and publishers.

COUNTRYSIDE BOOKS
3 Catherine Road
Newbury, Berkshire

To view our complete range of books please visit us at
www.countrysidebooks.co.uk

ISBN 978 1 84674 426 6

All materials used in the manufacture of this book carry FSC certification

Produced by The Letterworks Ltd., Reading
Designed and Typeset by KT Designs, St Helens
Printed by Holywell Press, Oxford

Contents

INTRODUCTION

Possessing a 90-mile coastline (stretching to 93 when the tide is out), Norfolk has one of the longest coastlines in the country. From long, windswept sandy beaches, to areas of deep shingle, dunes, cliffs and seaside resorts, it is a region of immense variety. Moving inland, there is an equally varied landscape crossed by heritage train routes, vast tracts of farmland, woods, forests, and heaths as well as the watery landscape of the Broads. For many people, the biggest surprise is discovering that Norfolk is not flat – this is an undulating landscape and hills do exist!

The good news for dog owners is that an increasing number of pubs in Norfolk are becoming dog friendly. Standards of food and drink have improved much in recent years, often focusing on local produce. All the pubs mentioned in this book are dog friendly, with some even providing doggy menus. Many are community pubs owned by the local inhabitants providing a focus for local life as well as being a pub, thus making them more resilient in the long term. Opening hours can vary by season, and should be checked before visiting.

All the walks listed here are between 1½ and 5 miles, although some like Weybourne's woodland and steam train exploration can be easily extended (or shortened) at various points along the way. Most are relatively easy going, suitable for any size of dog. The few exceptions possess some steeper walking sections where short-legged dogs might struggle. There are no stiles along the routes. However, some of the paths do get very muddy, with the occasional deep puddle, which my cocker spaniel companions quite enjoyed.

Above all, the real stars of this book are undoubtedly the hard working paws of cocker spaniels Freddie, Melodie, Maia, Jay, Indie and Merry, along with their humans Sarah and Bee. Always keen to try new walks, this cocker spaniel quintet loved exploring the byways, hidden pathways and beaches, remaining undaunted and happy throughout. They even shared one of their favourite walks around Burnham Market. Unfortunately, Freddie didn't make it to the end of me writing the book, as he sadly passed away. His enduring friendly welcome, wagging tail, constant looking back over his shoulder to make sure we were still there, and his determined paws will always be remembered. To Sarah, Bee and the doggy quintet for their unfailing friendship, patience and fun whatever the weather or location, my grateful thanks.

Thanks too to my husband Ian who was incredibly helpful sorting out pubs, and my daughter Karis, for her work navigating and taking photos.

Angela Youngman

PUBLISHER'S NOTE

We hope that you and your dog obtain considerable enjoyment from this book; great care has been taken in its preparation. In order to assist in navigation to the start point of the walk, we have included the nearest postcode, however, a postcode cannot always deliver you to a precise starting point, especially in rural areas. Although at the time of publication all routes followed public rights of way or permitted paths, diversion orders can be made and permissions withdrawn.

We cannot, of course, be held responsible for such diversion orders or any inaccuracies in the text which result from these or any other changes to the routes, nor any damage which might result from walkers trespassing on private property. We are anxious, though, that all the details covering the walks are kept up to date, and would therefore welcome information from readers which would be relevant to future editions.

The simple sketch maps that accompany the walks in this book are based on notes made by the author whilst surveying the routes on the ground. They are designed to show you how to reach the start and to point out the main features of the overall circuit, and they contain a progression of numbers that relate to the paragraphs of the text.

However, for the benefit of a proper map, we do recommend that you purchase the relevant Ordnance Survey sheet covering your walk – details of the relevant sheet are with each walk.

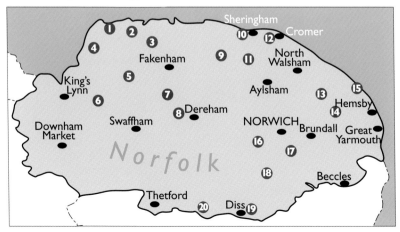

ADVICE FOR DOG WALKERS

The routes profiled in this book are designed to provide an enjoyable, stimulating walk for everyone, dog and human. They cover a variety of locations including links to steam trains, films, historic towns, woodland and open countryside. The Pulham Market walk even includes an opportunity to discover a lost heritage of airships.

When walking along country roads without pavements, for safety's sake, it is best to walk facing the traffic or on a grass verge if available. Take bags on every walk to remove dog poo. Wherever possible, the location of dog waste bins has been indicated on each walk, but not all walks have any such bins. Never leave bagged poo in the countryside – it will not degrade, and the plastic bags can cause problems for wildlife.

If walking on the beach it is very important to check tide times. Although the tide may go out a long way, leaving areas of sand dunes rising high, it can come back far quicker than many people expect creating dangerous situations in which people are left stranded by the incoming sea. Lifeboats are frequently called out to rescue walkers trapped among the sand dunes. Always keep watch on the sea, and be ready to head inland quickly before the tide turns. Knowing where your dog is at all times on a beach is essential for both your safety and that of your pet.

Equally important when walking on the beach or in the countryside is to observe any restrictions as to when dogs may or may not be allowed in certain areas. This may be due to resort requirements, or due to nesting birds.

Dogs should be kept on leads whenever they are near livestock. As most of these walks pass through open countryside, dog owners need to be aware of the possibility of encountering doggy distractions such as rabbits, hares, pheasants and other game birds as well as the occasional steam train. In springtime, sheep and lambs are frequently found in fields and dogs must be kept under control at all times. When exploring the coastline, there is a possibility that dogs may encounter seals and seal pups since many beaches, particularly on the east coast, are popular for breeding. Dogs should always be kept away from seals.

When walking in areas of bracken, fields or woodland, ticks can be a problem between spring and autumn. Ticks are blood-sucking parasites, which feed off livestock, birds and wild animals before dropping off and clinging to the undergrowth. After every walk, it is important to check your dog's fur since ticks may have attached themselves. Humans too can attract them, especially exposed legs and arms. An additional problem is that the ticks can cause Lyme disease, which can affect both humans and dogs. A serious illness with flu-like symptoms, it requires medical treatment before complications set in.

Any ticks that are found on your dog or yourself should be removed instantly since this reduces the risk of Lyme disease being transmitted. The best way to remove a tick is using a tick hook which is an inexpensive tool and worth purchasing. Alternatively, push tweezers or fingernails under the body of the tick close to the skin and pull the tick out without squeezing. Do not twist or pull the tick since this can leave the head and mouth in the skin. As long as the head and mouth are attached to the skin, the risk of infection remains.

Seasonal Canine Disease was first identified in Norfolk on the Sandringham Estate. It is a very serious illness, causing severe diarrhoea and vomiting within 24 to 48 hours of infection. Research into the disease is still underway, and no one knows the cause. Possible suggestions have included mites, virus and bacteria. This disease has been encountered at Sandringham and Thetford Forest. Neither location is close to any of the walks within this book, but if you think your dog may have any symptoms after walking in woodland areas, you must take your dog to a vet immediately.

1 THORNHAM
4 miles (6.4 km)

An attractive village, Thornham is situated within the Norfolk Coast Area of Outstanding Natural Beauty. It is separated from the sea by large areas of salt marsh and lies between two major bird reserves: RSPB Titchwell Marsh and Holme Dunes National Nature Reserve. Dogs can pass through part of the nature reserve, but must be kept under close control, especially during nesting season. This makes a pleasant walk with its combination of marshes, sand dunes, beach and quiet roads offering lots of variety. Near Holme, it is possible to see the beach where Seahenge, a prehistoric monument resembling Stonehenge but comprising a large tree stump buried upside down with roots in the air, surrounded by smaller tree trunks, was discovered at the turn of this century.

Start & Finish: Church Street, Thornham. **Sat Nav:** PE36 6NJ.
Parking: Roadside parking is available on Church Street outside the church. Alternatively, both pubs have good-sized car parks available for patrons.
Map: OS Explorer 250 Norfolk Coast West. **Grid ref:** TF733434.

THE PUB

THE ORANGE TREE has an award-winning restaurant with accommodation attached. Dogs are welcome in the bar where water bowls are available, and they even have their own doggy menu. Dogs can stay with their owners

in the ground floor bedrooms for an extra charge.
☎ 01485 512213 ⊕ www.theorangetreethornham.co.uk

THE LIFEBOAT INN passed towards the end of the walk serves traditional pub fare made with locally-sourced ingredients.
☎ 01485 512236 ⊕ www.lifeboatinnthornham.com

Terrain: Footpaths, marshes, boardwalk, sand dunes, beach and quiet road. Keep watch on the tide if you are on the beach, as it is all too easy to be cut off by the incoming sea. There are three dog waste bins accessible on this walk. On parts of the walk dogs must be kept on a lead.
Nearest vets: Medivet 95 Westgate, Hunstanton, PE36 5EP.
☎ 01485 535950. Coastal Veterinary Group, 16 Ålma Road, Snettisham, PE31 7NY. ☎ 01485 544201.

The Walk

① With your back to the church, turn right and head along Church Street. Keep right at the little green with a fence on your left until you reach a signpost for the Norfolk Coast Path. Turn left and walk down the pathway

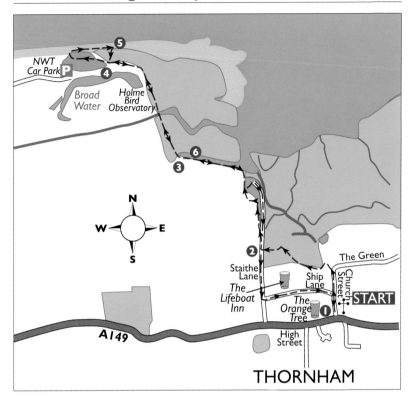

THORNHAM

until you reach the next footpath marker. Turn left again along the narrow footpath through the reed beds – this path is marked by an acorn sign and can get muddy in the winter or after heavy rain. Dogs are best kept on a lead in this area.

2 At the end, turn right onto a small road following the Norfolk Coast Path sign. Cars are often parked along this road so take care. Almost immediately you then head up the slope on the left-hand side of the road, leading to a raised walkway. This is part of the Norfolk Coast Path which you follow for ½ mile. The route passes through the Holme Dunes National Nature Reserve. Dogs and humans are requested to stay on the footpath except where there is a clear pathway leading down onto the dunes.

3 When you reach the next junction keep ahead to continue walking along the main path towards Holme-next-the-Sea. Part of this route involves a wooden boardwalk, which is uneven in places. The route crosses salt marshes, with Broad Water on the left. This lake forms part of the Holme Bird Observatory.

4 At the end of the boardwalk, the footpath widens out and leads through a forest. Dogs must remain on the path within three metres of their owners. When you reach the next signpost, there is a choice of two options. You can turn left towards the Holme Dunes Visitor Centre, which contains toilets, food and drink; then retrace your steps. Or, unless the tide is in, turn right towards the beach, then right again to walk along the beach. Dogs must be kept away from flocks of birds, or the roped off areas close to the sand dunes when ground nesting birds are present. Apart from this restriction, dogs can be safely let off the lead, and allowed to run freely on the wide sandy beach, and to paddle in the sea.

Take care on the beach as the tide can turn very quickly, leaving people and dogs marooned on sandbanks by the incoming tide.

5 In 200 metres you reach a Norfolk Wildlife Trust sign on the right. It is not possible to walk all the way back along the beach to Thornham itself. Turn right at the sign and follow the path through the dunes until you reach the steps leading back up to the Norfolk Coast Path boardwalk. Turn left retracing your steps back towards Thornham. You can follow the lower path on the left-hand side of the raised path – but this can get very muddy and wet in winter.

6 Continue retracing your steps until you reach a turning to the left, leading across a sluice gate. Take this turning and walk towards the car park on the far side. Turn right and follow this narrow access road for around 300 metres until you reach Ship Lane. Turn left, passing the Lifeboat Inn, and at the end of the road turn right back towards the church and your car. For the Orange Tree keep ahead to the High Street and turn right.

2 BRANCASTER STAITHE

2¾ miles (4.5 km)

Brancaster Staithe is a coastal village located within a designated Area of Outstanding Natural Beauty. Once a busy port, trade declined in the 1800s but today it still has a thriving local fishing industry and is a popular tourist destination. Much of the area is in the care of the National Trust including the marshes and the ancient Roman military fort known as Branodunum. The Norfolk Coast Path runs through Brancaster Staithe, and forms part of this circular walk through the marshes and across Barrow Common, which is a popular route with walkers. Large sections of this walk are ideal for dogs to be let off the lead for a run, especially on the Common.

Start & Finish: The Jolly Sailors, Main Road, Brancaster Staithe.
Sat Nav: PE31 8BJ.
Parking: Park at the Jolly Sailors if visiting, but please ask permission before leaving your car. Alternatively, park roadside on Orchard Close, just off Common Lane.
Map: OS Explorer 250 Norfolk Coast West. **Grid ref:** TF793442.

THE PUB THE JOLLY SAILORS is a large 18th-century, award-winning village pub where muddy paws are definitely welcome.

Dogs are allowed in the bar area as well as in the garden, which has several brightly coloured beach huts. It is well known for its excellent home-cooked food, large selection of rums and local real ales brewed at their own microbrewery.

☎ 01485 210314 ⊕ www.jollysailorsbrancaster.co.uk

Terrain: Quiet country roads, gentle gradients, open common and marshes, historic sites. There are dog waste bins on Barrow Common and at the end of Cross Lane.
Nearest vets: Medivet 95 Westgate, Hunstanton, PE36 5EP. ☎ 01485 535950. Coastal Veterinary Group, Creake Road, Burnham Market, PE31 8EA. ☎ 01485 544201.

The Walk

1 Head up the quiet country road (Common Road) to the right of the Jolly Sailors. This has a gentle hilly gradient and no footpath, but there are grass banks on either side edged by hedges. In around ½ mile you will reach Barrow Common at the top of the hill. Pass a bench on the left with a sign for the common and, a little further on, turn right onto a well-defined path through thick gorse bushes. Continue walking straight ahead, ignoring any side paths. Pass through a gate marked with a dog poo sign requesting 'Use stick to flick into thicket'. Below the sign is a pink striped spade. There are seats at various points ideal for enjoying the view (or allowing the dogs to take a rest!).

2 In around ¼ mile the path reaches a patch of trees, and winds slightly to the right heading downwards. At the bottom of the path, pass through the gate. There is a signpost clearly marking the path direction on the far side of the gate marked 'Brancaster Staithe circular walk'. Continue walking down the wide, hedge-lined path. Looking ahead, there are extensive

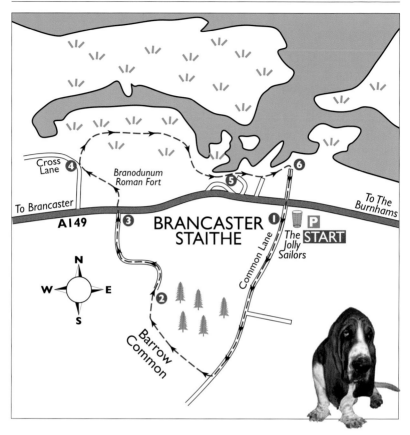

views across the Brancaster Marshes to the North Sea. At the bottom of the path follow the signpost pointing left and then keep going as it winds right and ends at a road.

❸ Cross the road, and head through a gap in the hedge opposite leading towards the remains of Branodunum Roman Fort. At the end of the field, turn left, then right at the gate. Head left towards the road where you will find a dog waste bin if needed.

❹ On your right you'll see a National Trust signed gateway (also part of the Fort). Livestock may be in the field, so dogs should be kept on the lead. Continue walking straight ahead, towards the trees at the bottom of the field. Pass through the next gate. Turn right onto a narrow raised boardwalk which leads across the marshes. The boardwalk is covered with netting ensuring it is safe to use all year round, although take extra care in the winter when the soil can be waterlogged and marshy. Keep walking ahead along this straight path for around ¾ mile.

⑤ Passing through the gate, the path divides to the right and left. Take the left-hand turning (the right-hand turn leads back to the main road), skirting the grassy area and curving behind a series of buildings and continue to follow signs for Brancaster Staithe circular walk. You will cross another roadway with the harbour car park on your left and activity centre on your right. Continue to follow the waymarked signs. There are good views of the creeks and lakes of the marshes, in which boats may be seen moored or in use.

⑥ At Brancaster Staithe Quay there is a signpost pointing right towards the Jolly Sailors public house. Turn right and walk ahead for about 150 metres and the car park can be seen directly across the road.

3 BURNHAM THORPE
3¼ miles (5.2 km)

The River Burn runs through the centre of the village, which is in a very quiet, rural location surrounded by open fields. This is primarily a crop growing area, although livestock such as pigs and horses may sometimes be present. Vice Admiral Horatio Nelson, victor of the Battle of Trafalgar, was born at Burnham Thorpe in September 1758. His father was rector of All Saints' Church where young Horatio was baptised. As a child, Nelson learned to sail in the network of rivers and creeks around Burnham Thorpe, before joining the Royal Navy in 1770, aged 12. Nelson returned to Burnham Thorpe on numerous occasions, living here with his wife between 1786 and 1793, as a half pay officer on the Royal Navy reserve list while waiting to be assigned to a ship. The site of his birthplace can still be seen in the village, as there is a plaque on a garden wall.

Start & Finish: The Lord Nelson, Walsingham Road, Burnham Thorpe.
Sat Nav: PE31 8HL.
Parking: Park at the Lord Nelson if visiting, but please ask permission before leaving your car. Alternatively, park roadside outside the church on Church Lane and start the walk at point 2.
Map: OS Explorer 250 Norfolk Coast West. **Grid ref:** TF852414.

THE PUB **THE LORD NELSON** was built in 1637 but originally traded as the Plough until in 1798 it was renamed following Horatio Nelson's victory at the Battle of the Nile. A whitewashed building on the edge of the village, it is owned by the Holkham Estate and was renovated throughout in 2020. Wooden settles (including one used by Nelson) provide iconic seating. The family-friendly menu contains plenty of locally produced pub favourites and dogs are welcome in the bar area and attractive garden. ☎ 01328 854988. ⊕ www.nelsonslocal.com

Terrain: There is often livestock within the area, as well as many ground nesting birds during the spring and summer so dogs should be kept on leads. Mostly flat terrain, although some of the paths can be a bit rough underfoot. Low gradients, mainly flat but rough field paths and quiet country lanes. There is a dog bin for dog waste situated on the edge of Lowes Lane, beside the river. **Nearest vets:** Coastal Veterinary Group, 16 Creake Road, Burnham Market, PE31 8EA. ☎ 01485 544201. Glaven Veterinary Practice, The Old Mill, Maryland, Wells-next-the-Sea, NR23 1LY. ☎ 01328 711022.

The Walk

. . . .

❶ Turn left on leaving the pub car park then take the next right-hand turn, along a quiet road. Cross over the River Burn and keep following the road round to the right until you reach the church.

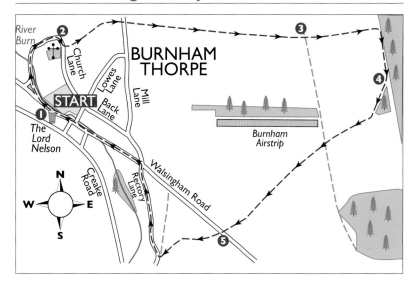

2 As the road curves to the right again, take the wide field path immediately straight ahead. A public bridleway, this path, with trees and hedges on the left-hand side, opens out to provide splendid views across the fields. In ¼ mile you reach a crossroads, where you follow the path straight ahead. This is a long, hedge-lined, straight path along the edge of open fields. It can be quite exposed to wind and rain and in wet weather there can be lots of puddles, some of which are quite deep – perfect for dogs who enjoy splashing through the water.

3 This path ends at another crossroads, with a stone built barn on the right-hand side. Cross the road, and follow the path ahead, past the barn and heading towards a small wood in the distance. Turn right when you reach the long stone wall surrounding the Holkham Hall estate. Follow the line of the wall until you reach a signpost showing three arrows pointing to different walking paths.

4 Turn right here. At the end of the woodland follow the path round to the right keeping the hedge to your left. Keep ahead until you reach a bend in a wider farm track on the edge of a pig farm. Turn left and walk along this farm track for just under ½ mile until you reach a crossroads.

5 Cross straight over onto a narrow lane. In ¼ mile you will reach another lane where you turn right. The village can be seen in the distance. Keep walking ahead until you reach Walsingham Road. Turn left and head into the village of Burnham Thorpe passing signs for Nelson's birthplace. In the winter, after periods of heavy rain, this road may be flooded. You can continue walking along the road towards the Lord Nelson, or take the small wooden bridge over the river to stroll along the grassy common ending at a dog waste bin on your right, at the edge of Lowes Lane. Turn left, then right to rejoin Walsingham Road.

4 RINGSTEAD
5 miles (8.3 km)

Ringstead is a small village high on the Ringstead Downs, an area of Special Scientific Interest. This is a very tranquil route leading through undulating open countryside, part of which includes the ancient Peddars Way – a long-distance footpath starting at Knettishall Heath near Thetford and ending at Holme-next-the-Sea, on the North Norfolk coast. The trail dates back to Celtic and Roman times and was used extensively by travellers and traders. During the Medieval period it was renamed Peddars Way in honour of the pilgrims who used it when walking to Walsingham, a famous pilgrimage site south of Ringstead. Long straight paths make this route quite easy to follow, giving time to enjoy the scenery and bird song. Dogs can be safely let off the lead for much of the walk.

Start & Finish: The Gin Trap, 6 High Steet, Ringstead.
Sat Nav: PE36 5JU.
Parking: Park at the Gin Trap if visiting, but please ask permission before leaving your car. Alternatively, park roadside along the High Street.
Map: OS Explorer 250 Norfolk Coast West. **Grid ref:** TF707403.

THE PUB **THE GIN TRAP** is a traditional 17th-century coaching inn on the main high street. Well behaved dogs are allowed inside the cosy bar area, where the tables are on a first-come first-served basis, and at bookable tables in the conservatory and garden. Food is sourced locally and the bar stocks over 100 different gins.

☎ 01485 525264 ⊕ www.thegintrapinn.co.uk

THE GIN TRAP INN

Terrain: Dogs can be safely let off the lead on the long, straight paths passing through cultivated fields. The route does include some local roads but the majority of the walk is along field paths. There is a dog bin near the pub, and more along the way.

Nearest vets: Medivet, 95 Westgate, Hunstanton, PE36 5EP.
☎ 01485 535950.

The Walk

....

① Turn left as you leave the pub car park. Cross over, and follow the main road as it curves round to the left. Keep straight ahead along Docking Road, passing a large oak tree on the left-hand side. Follow the road as it bears round to the right. In 200 metres the road turns sharply to the left, with a lane directly ahead. Follow the lane marked by a signpost highlighting the Ringstead circular walks, and a sign for Peddars Way South. On the left-hand side there are some houses with a large natural pond opposite which is usually occupied by a large flock of ducks. The lane becomes a track leading between hedges and fields which can be a bit rough and muddy in places. Ignore the turning on the left leading towards some farm buildings and head through a gate continuing along the path marked Peddars Way. Long hedgerows border the path and contain lots of brambles, providing delicious fruit for picking in the late summer and autumn.

2 After about a mile the path opens out onto an unmade road where you turn left. There is a signpost marking the route to take. Walk past some old pump house buildings until you reach a road (Docking Road again). Cross over the road following the signs opposite for Courtyard Farm. Immediately

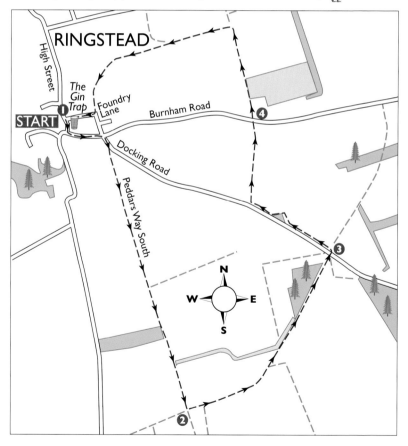

to your left you will see a signpost for a footpath passing through fields. In the early summer, these fields contain a blaze of red poppies.

3 Head along the field edge which runs parallel with Docking Road. The path is a long, straight track, wide enough for two people and dogs to walk side-by-side. It heads slightly uphill, passing through fields. There are wide verges on either side filled in summer with wild flowers such as oxeye daisies, field scabious, cornflower, yarrow, red campion and corn marigolds. Larks have been heard singing high overhead, and red kites can sometimes be seen circling in the sky. You will reach a small wood on the left-hand side of the path, with a field opening ahead. Go straight through the field opening and keep to the left along the edge of the field. The path leads downwards and round to the right, passing through a narrow gate. Follow the path through two more gates until you reach a road (Burnham Road).

4 Cross over Burnham Road and follow the wide path directly ahead until you reach a path to your left. Take this path past Bluestone Farm and round to the left. It will lead you to Foundry Lane where you turn right back to the pub.

5 GREAT MASSINGHAM

4 miles (6.4 km)

Great Massingham is a very pretty village, with three deep duck ponds of which two are located beside the large village green. The village is believed to date back to the 5th century, although the duck ponds were originally fish ponds for an 11th-century Augustinian Abbey which was located in the area. This meandering walk, with frequent twists and turns passes through fields, woods and even an old airbase. Although the paths are rutted in places and can be a little overgrown especially in high summer, both you and your dog should enjoy this peaceful walk. Dogs can be let off the lead for part of the route.

Start & Finish: The Dabbling Duck, 11 Abbey Road, Great Massingham.
Sat Nav: PE32 2HN.
Parking: Park at the Dabbling Duck if visiting, but please ask permission before leaving your car. Alternatively, there is roadside parking right outside the pub around the green.
Map: OS Explorer 250 Norfolk Coast West. **Grid ref:** TF797228.

THE PUB THE DABBLING DUCK is owned by local farmers, and the frequent presence of the manager's black Labrador highlights the dog friendly nature of this pub. A great place to eat and relax after a long walk, the food is sourced locally and prepared on site. A traditional village pub facing onto the green, it is friendly and relaxing, while in the winter the big open fire makes it very warm and cosy. The pub is open for breakfast, making it a good location for early morning walks especially in the summer when dogs can enjoy a long walk before it gets too hot. Dogs are welcome in most areas of the pub, although it may not be possible in some parts of the restaurant.
☎ 01485 520827 ⊕ www.thedabblingduck.co.uk

There is also an excellent dog friendly tearoom opposite called **The Cartshed**, along with a general store.

Terrain: Dog bins can be found close to the Dabbling Duck car park, near the Primary School, at two T-junctions along the route as well as in Mill Lane.
Nearest vets: Swaffham Veterinary Centre , Unit 3 Tower Meadows, Swaffham, PE37 7LT. ☎ 01760 722054.

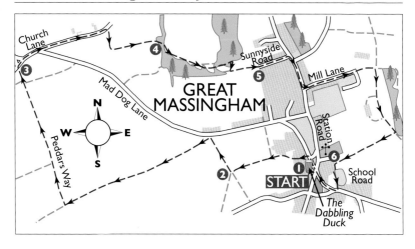

The Walk

1 Turn left out of the Dabbling Duck, passing a dog bin. Just past Duckling Cottage, there is a signpost marking a footpath on the left-hand side of the road. Turn left along this wide footpath, walking on soil and grass, passing a house and outbuildings, and alongside fields. The path eventually narrows, and another footpath marker comes into view. Continue walking straight on, following the long straight path between fields and hedges. It can be a little uneven in places with hidden ruts.

2 At the T-junction turn right, and then at the next T-junction turn left onto a concrete road leading between tall hedges and heading towards the radio transmitters in the distance. A dog bin can be seen on the right-hand side. Just past the radio transmitters, the path reaches another T-junction, facing a signpost, where you turn right onto the Peddars Way. This is a rough, stony path with an open field on the left-hand side. Beware, it can get very wet and muddy as there are some quite large potholes in places – which dogs quite enjoy jumping into! Follow the path along the field edge for around ½ mile.

3 On reaching the T-junction, turn right onto Church Lane, a quiet local road with a wide grass verge. This leads past the entrance to a farm on the left-hand side. Pass an open gateway into a field opposite the farm to reach a footpath sign on your right. Turn right onto the footpath leading towards a field, and then turn sharp right onto a wooded path. Follow the footpath as it winds to the left, and look

for an opening on the left, between two trees, which leads onto a field path. Keep along the edge of a cultivated arable field aiming for the trees ahead.

4 Go through the somewhat overgrown gap in the wooded hedge. The path emerges into the next field. Follow the track across the field to reach the opening in the hedge directly ahead. Go through the gap in the hedge, and keep to the path as it winds through trees and undergrowth to the edge of a paddock. Follow the path as it turns right along the fence line. During late summer and autumn, tall nettles can be a problem along this section of the path. Ignore the disused stiles on the left and walk on, past a large house in the distance.

The path veers to the right, leading to a gateway marked by a concrete stump on the left and a wooden stump on the right. Walk through the gateway into the field and turn left. Continue walking along the edge of the field, following the track as it leads away from the trees towards houses in the distance. There is a hedge on one side, and open cultivated field on the other.

5 On reaching the end of the public footpath, a dog bin can be found on the left, beside a public footpath sign. Walk straight ahead on a paved path beside a residential road (Sunnyside Road). At the T-junction, turn right into Station Road and then turn left into Mill Lane. Just past the row of houses, there is a dog bin on the left-hand side, beside a field. Keep walking along the tree-lined concrete track, past the entry to a small industrial estate on the right and through a gap between two large tree trunks set on their sides. The route takes you through a former Second World War airfield operated by the RAF until the 1950s. At the T-junction, turn right and walk straight ahead keeping the large barn on your right. Towards the end of the runway, look for a public footpath sign on the right-hand side. Turn right onto this narrow grassy path leading between a hedge and a paddock with Great Massingham church tower seen in the distance. Keep walking straight ahead.

6 When you reach the end of the path, turn left and follow the path between trees and the local primary school. A dog bin can be found at the end of the path. At the road, turn right and walk towards the V-shaped road junction. Keep right along School Road, past the duck pond and you'll soon see the Dabbling Duck across the green to your left.

6 SHOULDHAM WARREN

3¼ miles (5.3 km)

Shouldham is a small village with a traditional green set amid gently rolling countryside. Shouldham Warren is a nature reserve incorporating woodland walks and a rhododendron avenue, which offers lots of colour in the springtime, while in the autumn the deciduous trees provide brilliant autumn hues. The name Shouldham Warren reflects the long history of rabbit farming in the area. During the medieval period, warrens were set as a way of breeding and nurturing supplies of rabbits for meat and fur, which was a major industry in the area until the 19th century. Rabbits continue to play a major role ensuring the conservation of this individualistic, biodiverse region. Walkers and horse riders use the trails extensively all year round as the well-drained soil creates firm walking surfaces.

Start & Finish: The King's Arms, 28 The Green, Shouldham.
Sat Nav: PE33 0BY.
Parking: Park at the King's Arms if visiting, but please ask permission before leaving your car. Alternatively, park roadside around the village green.
Map: OS Explorer 236 King's Lynn, Downham Market & Swaffham.
Grid ref: TF677088.

THE PUB — **THE KING'S ARMS** was one of the first community-owned pubs to be opened in the UK. Since then the award-winning pub has steadily increased the services it provides to the village, holding regular events as well as running a community shop. The pub is known for its real ale with beer sourced from local breweries. The food menu changes regularly, and always includes locally produced food. There is a large outside seating area, part of which comprises a covered patio. Dogs are welcome inside, and there is always a bowl of water and a dog biscuit available for four-legged friends. Check the website for opening times.

☎ 01366 347410 ⊕ www.kingsarmshouldham.co.uk

Terrain: Hard-surfaced footpaths, field tracks, woodland trails and a short section of road. Dog waste bins are available close to the start of the walk, at the entrance to the car park at the far side of Shouldham Warren, and then again close to the end of the walk. Well-behaved dogs can be let off leads for most of this walk. There are lots of side paths that can be taken while in Shouldham Warren enabling the walk to be extended to become as long as dogs need.

Nearest vets: Vets One Group, Home Farm Barns, Downham Road, Crimplesham, PE33 9DU. ☎ 01366 384644.

The Hollies Veterinary Clinic, 29 Paradise Road, Downham Market, PE38 9JE. ☎ 01366 386655.

The Walk

• •

❶ With your back to the pub entrance, cross the road and walk diagonally across the village green, past the phone box towards the footpath that can be seen between two houses almost directly opposite the King's Arms. Follow the hard surfaced path straight ahead. It winds to the right behind some houses until it divides into two, just where there is a dog waste bin. Turn left and

follow the grassy path until you reach Westgate Street.

❷ Turn right and head along Westgate Street for around 100 metres, then take the turning to your left marked Orchard Lane. The hard surfaced path ends at a house driveway, which is covered in a thick layer of gravel. The footpath continues across the driveway, and round to the left and develops into a narrow gravel path between a fence and field, before changing to a grass and soil path beside an overgrown stream on the left. This is a narrow path, wide enough for one person and a dog, which can get very muddy during the winter. Leads are recommended at this point. The path ends at a T-junction where you turn right following the farm track through fields. This is a much wider path and is used by farm vehicles.

③ On reaching another T-junction, turn right along a wide path which is full of ruts. In winter and after heavy rain, it is very muddy with deep puddles.

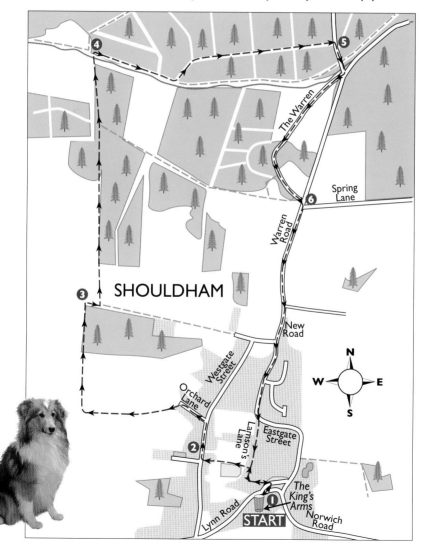

In 60 metres turn left at the signpost, following the well drained, wooded, track into Shouldham Warren. This is a straight track with numerous unmarked side paths – perfect for exploring if you have a large dog needing a longer walk. In late spring, there are rhododendrons in bloom. Keep walking straight ahead until you reach Black Drain, a deep V-shaped drain, with an unfenced trackway leading across it.

4 Turn right, and follow the wide path edged by trees and undergrowth on the left-hand side. Dogs can be off leads in this area, although you do need to watch for them trying to go down towards the water flowing through Black Drain. In ¼ mile the path divides with one branch going off to the left. Take this left-hand turning which winds upwards through the wood. At the next junction turn right onto a wide path, well used by dog walkers and horse riders. The terrain opens out becoming more of an open common, with large expanses of heather as well as trees and woodland. Keep walking straight ahead.

5 Turn right at the next T-junction, heading down towards a car park. There is a dog waste bin at the entrance to the car park. Walk through the car park and over Black Drain towards the woodland path on the right-hand side.

Turn right here and follow the path round to the left past some houses until you reach a road junction with a 'Give Way' sign.

⑥ Turn right down Warren Road which leads you back into the village of Shouldham. This is a quiet country road with wide grassy banks to walk along. Follow the road for ½ mile, past the houses and until it curves round to the left. At this point, the entrance to a footpath marked Lamson's Lane can be seen straight ahead. Take this well-maintained footpath passing the back of houses. Initially mainly grassy, it becomes a hard surfaced path leading back to where the footpath first diverged at the start of the walk. Pass a dog waste bin on the right-hand side and continue walking straight ahead as the path winds to the left. Retrace your steps across the green to reach the pub.

7 BEESTON

2½ miles (3.8 km)

Beeston is a pretty village set amid open countryside between Dereham, Fakenham and King's Lynn. It is sometimes known as Beeston All Saints or Beeston-next-Mileham in order to distinguish it from other Norfolk villages bearing the same name. A tranquil village, it is surrounded by farmland as well as the nearby Beeston auction house. Jets from RAF Marham located to the south of the A47 can often be seen practicing in the sky.

Although this is a walk involving roads, all are local and traffic is minimal. There are lots of grass verges, as well as occasional pavements within Beeston village. It makes a very good winter walk, although enjoyable whatever the season.

> **Start & Finish:** The Beeston Ploughshare, The Street, Beeston.
> **Sat Nav:** PE32 2NF.
> **Parking:** Park at the Beeston Ploughshare, but please ask permission before leaving your car.
> **Map:** OS Explorer 238 Dereham & Aylsham. **Grid ref:** TF904158.

THE PUB

THE BEESTON PLOUGHSHARE is a popular community-owned pub which reopened in 2019 after extensive refurbishment undertaken by the villagers. A friendly, welcoming pub it has a large comfortable bar with an inglenook fireplace plus a separate dining room with an additional

small room off the bar which doubles as a café during the day. Also on site is a small shop providing day-to-day essentials. Outside there is a large patio area surrounded by pretty planting. Traditional English meals are available in the bar and the dining room. Beeston Brewery is just down the road, and there is always at least one of their beers available at the bar. Dogs are very welcome here, with water bowls provided. ☎ 01328 598995 ⊕ www.beestonploughshare.com

---

Terrain: Flat, firm terrain along roadsides with some pavements. As this is a walk involving numerous roads, dogs are best kept on leads. There are two dog bins available at different points within the walk; at the turning towards Fransham and near the top of Dairy Drift.
Nearest vets: Larwood & Kennedy Veterinary Practice, 7 Wellington Road, Dereham, NR19 2BP. ☎ 01362 692508.

The Walk

. . . .

❶ Turn left out of the pub car park, and walk along the quiet village road through the centre of the village. There is no pavement at this point. In 200 metres the road merges onto Church Road where open countryside with young woodland and open fields, cultivated with crops, appears on either side of the route. In the distance there are lovely views of a church steeple rising high above the tree line and sections of mixed hedging, with brambles, blackthorn, wild roses and hawthorn.

❷ In just over ¼ mile the road reaches a triangle of grass marking a left-hand turn which you take. There is a signpost towards Fransham, as well as a bin for dog waste. Cultivated farmland broken by patches of trees and tall hedges can be seen on both sides of the road. A deep ditch appears for a short while on the left-hand side and there are wide grassy verges. The sweet aroma of hops and beer on the air marks the location of the Beeston Brewery, also known as Fransham Road Farm. This is a local real ale brewery, and their beer can be enjoyed at the Ploughshare pub in Beeston.

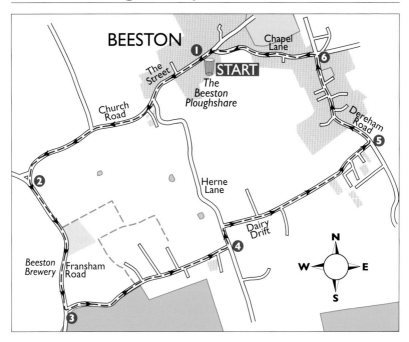

③ Just beyond Beeston Brewery take the turning on the left-hand side of the road, directly opposite a signpost almost hidden in the hedge on your right, heading towards Wendling. Continue to walk straight ahead past hedges and fields with the occasional jet from RAF Marham overhead, or heard in the distance.

④ In around ½ mile you reach a T-junction marked with a signpost. Turn left, then immediately right into Dairy Drift passing a solar farm on the left. There is a wide grassy verge and blackberries to be found in the hedgerows in season. The road is very straight and passes between hedges and cultivated farmland. Towards the top of the road there is an easily overlooked dog bin hidden in the hedge on the right. Continue walking ahead past the entrance to a distribution company and Beeston Auctions.

⑤ When you reach the T-junction, turn left. This road can be much busier in terms of traffic but it is only a short distance before it enters the village. There is a wide grass verge on the left-hand side beside the open field. On entering the village of Beeston, continue walking straight ahead, past an old well on the right-hand side. There are no pavements, but it is a quiet road. At the end of the village, there is a crossroads with Beeston Primary School on the right, and a village sign on the left. The village sign is very decorative highlighting Beeston's agricultural history and links to the Second World War airfield that used to exist in this area.

6 Turn left into Chapel Lane, walking past houses and a weather vane with a bomber beside a barn. There is a pavement for much of the way. At the T-junction with Back Lane, turn left into The Street heading towards Litcham, before turning left again into the Ploughshare pub car park.

8 GRESSENHALL
4½ miles (7.3 km)

The origins of the village name are uncertain, but some sources believe it could mean a 'grassy area'. This is a region of arable fields, woodland and small villages connected by a network of paths and quiet lanes. This circular walk explores some of these paths linking Gressenhall and Beetley and covers tracks and quiet roads, passing through open countryside and woodland. Much of this walk is best undertaken with dogs kept on leads. However, the woodland is great for dogs to explore – as are the muddy puddles! This route offers a good variety of smells and terrain, which dogs should enjoy.

Start & Finish: The White Swan, The Green, Gressenhall.
Sat Nav: NR20 4DU.
Parking: Park at the White Swan if visiting, but please ask permission before leaving your car. Alternatively, there is roadside parking just by the pub around the village green.
Map: OS Explorer 238 Dereham & Aylsham. **Grid ref:** TF964165.

THE PUB

THE WHITE SWAN is a community-owned inn on the edge of Gressenhall village. The food on offer is varied, focusing on seasonal home-cooked dishes using primarily local produce. Teas, coffee and cakes are always available along with a choice of beers, many from local breweries. Dogs are welcome in the bar and there is always a bowl of fresh water waiting.
☎ 01362 861296 ⊕ www.thewhiteswangressenhall.co.uk

> **Terrain:** Mix of pavements, quiet lanes with verges, woodland, bridleways and field paths. Dogs can be let off the lead along the various bridleways and quiet lanes, although care needs to be taken whenever the path reaches a busier road. There is a dog bin located towards the end of the walk, on the B1146 in Beetley.
> **Nearest vets:** Larwood & Kennedy Veterinary Practice, 7 Wellington Road, Dereham, NR19 2BP. ☎ 01362 692508.

The Walk

❶ Turn left out of the pub car park, and cross over the main road heading towards Bittering Street opposite and slightly to your left. This is a quiet residential road, with a footpath for part of the way. When the footpath ends, there is a wide verge. In less than ½ mile you reach a crossroads where you turn left along Longham Lane. It is a narrow lane, very firm underfoot with a hard tarmac surface and grass verges. In 100 metres, opposite Manor Farm, there is another signpost where you turn right onto the Nar Valley Way. A quiet, peaceful but well-used bridleway, this is a long, narrow grassy path passing between hedges and trees. There are lots of wild roses, holly, brambles, elders and nettles to be seen. At times the terrain can be a little uneven due to tree roots protruding from the earth, or ruts in the path. A ditch can be seen on the left of the winding trackway, and eventually you pass a large pond. There is no access for dogs as it is quite a steep drop below the side of the path. Glimpses of open agricultural land can be seen in places along the way. Towards the end of the path, the surface becomes very raised in the centre, and there are traces of tractor wheels which can make for rough walking.

❷ In ¾ mile the path comes to an end at a narrow country lane. A very deep and large puddle was discovered stretching across the entire path last time I walked this route, but Melody and Maia immediately enjoyed a paddle! Turn right onto Stoney Lane with hedges and arable fields on both sides. In around ½ mile you reach a crossroads, where you

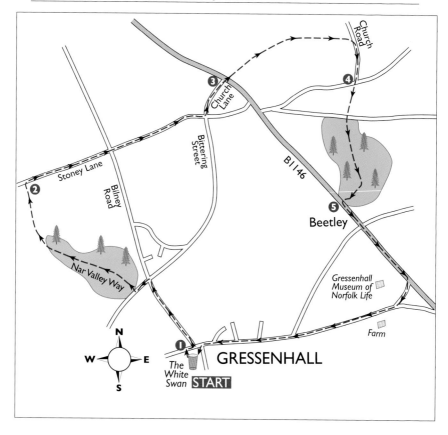

cross over and continue ahead. At the next crossroads, just after Vale Farm, turn left along Church Lane, signed towards East Bilney.

The quiet lane winds to the right passing through an area of woodland, but leads ultimately to the B1146, a busy road.

3 Cross over the road and walk straight ahead along the trackway opposite. It leads through arable fields and large expanses of bracken and can get very muddy in places. Continue walking ahead, aiming for the church tower that appears in the distance. Eventually you reach the end of the track at a T-junction with houses and the church to the left. Turn right into Church Road and walk ahead until you reach a junction.

4 Ignore the lane to the left and start to follow the road round to the right. Ahead you will see a footpath sign by an opening into a field. Follow this narrow path across the edge of an arable field, passing through an area

Nar Valley Way
Restricted Byway

of open countryside. It ends at a small area of undergrowth and trees which leads to a quiet road. Cross over and continue walking straight ahead along the path between two houses before entering an area of deciduous woodland. This is a lovely part of the walk, which was much enjoyed by the dogs who could run off-lead and explore some small paths leading off to the side. A deep ditch appears on the left-hand side, together with a sign marked private woodland. The public footpath now winds to the right and becomes narrower, passing between a field on the left with a school in the distance, and a tall fence on the right-hand side. Continue ahead, until you reach the road at the bottom where you'll find a dog bin on the right.

5 Turn left along the B1146, and cross over to walk along the pavement through the village of Beetley, past houses and an area of trees. You will need to cross over again when the pavement switches sides. This is a busy road often used by vehicles, so take care. Continue walking straight ahead past the Gressenhall Museum of Norfolk Life, which can be seen on the right-hand side. Just past the museum, Litcham Road can be seen on the right, marked by a signpost for Gressenhall. Turn right and, keeping to the grass verges, continue walking straight ahead between fields owned by the museum, and a Victorian-style farm on the left. Animals can often be seen in these fields especially Suffolk Punch horses. The verges become a pavement as you reach an area of woodland which takes you into the village of Gressenhall. Keep ahead and in just over ¼ mile you will reach the White Swan.

9 HOLT & SPOUT HILLS

2¾ miles (4.4 km)

The walk starts in the historic market town of Holt which dates back to Anglo Saxon times, but most of the centre was built in the 18th and early

19th century in Georgian style. Within the town, there is a wide range of independent shops, many of which are tucked away in quiet courtyards off the High Street. The route then explores Spout Hills which lie within the Glaven Valley, and are a Site of Special Scientific Interest, covering a 14-acre area of woodland and open grassland. Dogs can be safely let off leads and allowed to run and chase balls within much of the open countryside on the walk.

Start & Finish: The Feathers, Market Place, Holt.
Sat Nav: NR25 6BW.
Parking: Park at the Feathers in Holt if visiting, but please ask permission before leaving your car. Alternatively, park roadside along the High Street or in the large car park off Kerridge Way, and make your way through the alleyway to the High Street.
Map: OS Explorer 251 Norfolk Coast Central. **Grid ref:** TG078387.

THE PUB

THE FEATHERS offers special packages for overnight stays where dogs get their own doggy bed, towel and water bowl along with a welcome pack which includes a ball. This historic pub offers plenty of seating in the bar area complete with winter log fires and outdoor tables for warmer days. Part of the regional Chestnut Group of pubs, the company even has its own doggy related website, www.chestmutts.co.uk highlighting the various facilities and pawsome packages available.

☎ 01263 712318 ⊕ www.thefeathersholt.com

Terrain: Pavements, quiet roads, open countryside and woodland flint paths. There is a dog waste bin at the entrance to Spout Hills, at the exit from the Letheringsett Hill Car Park.
Nearest vets: Glaven Veterinary Practice, Oakland House, Old Station Way, Holt, NR25 6DH ☎ 01263 713200.

The Walk

● ●

❶ Turn left out of the pub, heading along the High Street until you reach a T-junction in around 200 metres. *This is marked by a black lamp post, the Queen Victoria Golden Jubilee Lantern and a pineapple-topped obelisk, which was originally one of a pair of gateposts from a nearby country estate but was given to the town in 1757.*

❷ Turn right, following the pavement down the hill for around 100 metres. Cross the road with care and turn left into Letheringsett Hill car park. A public footpath sign can be seen to your left pointing the way to Spout Hills and a dog waste bin is at the entrance. Follow the steep path downhill towards a pond in the distance. Dogs can be safely let off the lead in this area, and there is plenty of room for them to run and chase balls. Continue to follow the path keeping the pond on your left-hand side. When the path divides, follow the left-hand option down towards a stream, crossing it via one of the two flat concrete bridges. The path now leads steeply upwards. In winter, this area can get muddy.

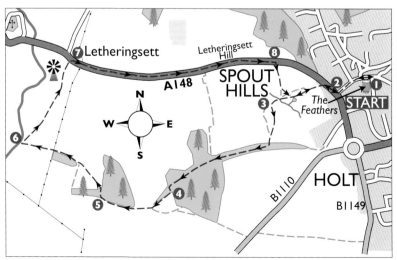

❸ The path soon winds to the left through open land. Keep walking straight ahead, until you reach a line of trees where you leave Spout Hills and join Norfolk County Council (NCC) public footpaths. Walk down a steep row of steps, and turn right at the bottom to follow the path marked by an NCC yellow arrow. This is a wide, flat tree-lined flint path with steep banks rising on either side. The ground steadily begins to drop away on either side, into deep hollows filled with deciduous woodland. The path continues straight ahead for just under ½ mile, flat and firm, marking the route of a disused railway line.

❹ Pass through the gap in the fence and, keeping the hedge to your right, follow the path as it winds to the right down to an open field. At the bottom, turn right along a field track, heading to the left of a small wood.

❺ When the path crosses another public footpath at a point marked by the telegraph wires overhead, turn right. The path steadily narrows between banks of ivy and bramble. At a point where three paths meet, follow the path winding to the right marked by a yellow NCC arrow. Walk straight ahead across the field. Trees will appear on the left and buildings can be seen in the distance straight ahead.

❻ The path emerges onto a concrete track. A ford with a bridge can be seen on the left. Dogs may enjoy exploring the ford, but beware that it can get deep

and unstable underfoot. Do not cross the ford. Instead, follow the concrete track to the right, keeping the tall stone wall on your left before passing houses as you walk into the village of Letheringsett. Just before you reach the T-junction, there is a turning to your left leading down to Letheringsett Watermill. This is a great place to stop for a visit to the tea room, flour shop and to explore the Mill Antiques and Brocante.

Returning to the road, you now have a choice. You can retrace your steps and return by the same path through the fields and disused railway line to Spout Hills. Alternatively, for a shorter circular option you can follow the A148 back towards the start.

7 If taking the road route, turn left after leaving the Letheringsett Watermill. At the T-junction, turn right following the concrete pavement. There is a wide green bank between the road and the pavement which leads uphill and can feel quite steep. Walk through the first lay-by and follow the path alongside the road on the narrow pavement. You will then reach a long lay-by marked by a stone wall on your right-hand side, used as a parking area for walkers visiting the Spout Hills. Continue walking to the far end where you will find a gateway on your right marked 'Welcome to the Spout Hills'.

8 Go through the gateway and walk ahead. At the junction, keep left along the level path towards the river and pond in the distance. This takes you back to the Letheringsett Hill car park entrance where you cross over the road and turn right. Turn immediately left to retrace your steps back through the centre of Holt to the Feathers pub.

10 WEYBOURNE
3½ or 5 miles (5.7 or 8 km)

Weybourne is a coastal village within the Norfolk Coast Area of Outstanding Natural Beauty and is surrounded by open countryside with fields, woodland and heathland. Although Norfolk is often described as being flat, this walk shows that the terrain can be very mixed, and involves some quite steep areas. There are also several alternative routes offering opportunities to lengthen or shorten the walk.

Part of the walk passes through Kelling Heath, an extensive area of woodland and heathland where there is an unmanned railway halt along the path. Here it is possible to join the Heritage Line to Weybourne, Holt and Sheringham, as long as a signal is given to the driver as the train approaches the halt. Some parts of the route are suitable for dogs to run off lead, but care needs to be taken anywhere near the trains.

Start & Finish: The Ship Inn, The Street, Weybourne.
Sat Nav: NR25 7SZ.
Parking: Park at the Ship Inn if visiting, but please ask permission before leaving your car. Alternatively, there is roadside parking on Beach Lane opposite the pub.
Map: OS Explorer 252 Norfolk Coast East. **Grid ref:** TG111431.

> **Terrain:** Woodland, heathland, hard surfaces, roads without pavements, tracks with some steep sections plus shingle beach. Dog waste bins can be found on Station Road, near All Saints Close, Weybourne, at the entrance to Weybourne Railway Station, on Kelling Heath near the Windpump Crossing.
> **Nearest vets:** Miramar Veterinary Centre, 15 Weybourne Road, Sheringham, NR26 8HF. ☎ 01263 822293.

THE PUB

THE SHIP INN is a large free house located in the centre of Weybourne. It is well known for its local ales and over 100 varieties of gin and has an extensive menu focusing on local and seasonal food, including seafood landed on Weybourne beach. Bar snacks and main meals are available, along with vegan, dairy free and gluten free options. There is a large bar complete with log burner, dining areas and a large garden. Overnight accommodation is also available. Dogs are allowed in the bar, dining area and garden but must be kept on leads at all times.
☎ 01263 588721 ⊕ www.theshipinnweybourne.com

The Walk

. . . .

❶ Leaving the pub, turn right and walk along the narrow pavement towards the church. Turn right into Church Street following the signs for Kelling Heath and the North Norfolk Railway, followed by a left-hand turn into Station Road. A long residential road winding steadily uphill, it contains lots of traditional flint buildings as well as more modern houses. There is a dog waste bin just after passing All Saints Close. The hard pavement continues after leaving the village, with the road now passing between fields and tall hedges. There are occasional views across the fields on the left, while the right-hand side offers uninterrupted field views. Trains can often be heard in the distance, especially the occasional whistle.

❷ In around 1 mile the pavement ends at the entrance to Weybourne Station. Here you can stop off at the station to see the trains, the allotment garden, have a coffee, explore the museum exhibits and see the platforms used by TV shows

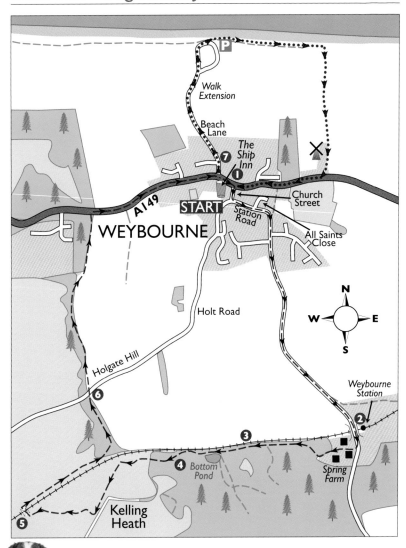

Walk Extension

Beach Lane

The Ship Inn

7

1

A149

START

Station Road

Church Street

WEYBOURNE

All Saints Close

P

Holt Road

N
W E
S

Holgate Hill

6

Weybourne Station

2

3

4 Bottom Pond

Spring Farm

5

Kelling Heath

like *Dad's Army*. A dog waste bin is located at the entrance to the platforms, and water for dogs is provided on the platforms. When you are ready to continue the walk, cross over the railway bridge directly ahead. Take care as there are no footpaths. Turn right beside Spring Farm where you'll find a public footpath leading through a gate heading towards Kelling Heath. Passing between hedges, the broad footpath leads to two gates marked private. The public footpath continues between the two gates, and becomes much narrower as it goes downhill. The footing underneath can be a bit rough, with tree

roots sticking up in places. This well-used path leads into Kelling Heath, an area of extensive deciduous woodland, and ultimately follows the line of the railway track.

3 In just under ½ mile you reach a viewpoint on the right-hand side, with three markers highlighting interesting landscape features. After leaving the viewpoint, the path descends downhill and becomes very rough underfoot. There are markers along the way identifying some of the trees as well as picnic benches opposite a sign for the North Norfolk Railway Kelling Halt. A large Bottom Pond appears on the left. This is a natural spring-fed pond, with the water constantly flowing, exiting by a manmade scrape under the tracks. Used as a fishing pond by children and beginners, it contains many aquatic plants and is fairly shallow, although it is 6 feet deep in the centre. Follow the path uphill, winding to the right towards the sign for Kelling Halt, the smallest station on the Holt-Sheringham North Norfolk Railway line. *An unmanned station, trains do not stop here on the way to Holt. It will stop for passengers on the return journey, providing a signal is given to the driver as the train comes into the station.* Walk to the far end of the platform to rejoin the woodland path on the left. This narrow path winds down into the woods, and becomes very meandering although still following the railway line, which is now higher than the path.

4 Soon after passing a field on the left, a marker post highlights two different routes. Both ultimately lead to the same path, but the right-hand path is much more difficult and probably only suitable for larger dogs. Follow the left-hand path which is sandy and wide, passing steeply uphill. At the top, turn right onto the track and continue walking ahead until you reach the railway line. A dog waste bin can be found on the right-hand side, about 100 metres after the narrow path merges with the wide one. Walk along the track until you reach a level crossing, known as Windpump Crossing.

5 Turn right and cross over the railway tracks, taking care to listen out for trains. Turn right again and follow the path back on the opposite side of the railway line. This is a straight path, with some ruts in places rising steadily towards a ridge in the distance and passing through a wide area of bracken, heather and gorse. At the ridge the path winds to the left away from the railway line, and begins to descend through the trees. Towards the bottom of the woods, the path winds to the left and becomes much narrower, meandering and undulating past field edges to the left. It comes to an end at a small country road (Holgate Hill) beside a public footpath sign.

6 Cross over the road and aim for the public footpath sign. This is a narrow woodland path, where it is often necessary to walk in single file. It passes through trees, under a natural holly tunnel, and skirts the edge of fields. A long path, it meanders, sometimes going uphill, sometimes downhill but is easy to follow and eventually emerges beside a public footpath marker on the Muckleburgh to Weybourne section of the A149 coastal road, directly opposite the Muckleburgh Collection. A sign for Kelling can be seen on the left. Turn right and follow the road (no footpath) back into Weybourne and the Ship Inn.

7 The walk can be extended down to the beach and windmill by heading down Beach Lane opposite the pub. This ends at a car park, with a shingle ridge at the far end. Climbing up the ridge provides access to the shingle leading down to the sea, with views of the wind farm in the distance. It is possible to walk along the shingle in either direction. Alternatively turn right, and follow the Norfolk Coast Path towards a row of coastguard cottages. Go through the gate and turn right towards the windmill to reach the main road. Turn right again and walk back through the village to reach the pub.

11 HEYDON

3 miles (4.6 km)

One of the last remaining privately owned villages in the UK, Heydon forms part of the Heydon Estate. This pretty village was mentioned in the Domesday Book of 1086, and there has been no new building in the village since 1887 when a well was built to commemorate Queen Victoria's Golden Jubilee. Dating back to the 14th century, the parish church of St Peter and St Paul contains a collection of medieval wall paintings. Heydon Hall is a Tudor mansion built in 1482, and has been in the ownership of the same family since the 17th century. According to legend, Oliver Cromwell was chased by a bull in the parkland and climbed an oak tree to escape. A tree known as Cromwell's Oak still stands in the park near the Hall. The surrounding countryside is agricultural and woodland which makes for an ideal dog walk.

Start & Finish: Heydon Village Car Park, The Street, Heydon.
Sat Nav: NR11 6AD.
Parking: Park in the village car park which is clearly signed on the approach to the village.
Map: OS Explorer 252 Norfolk Coast East. **Grid ref:** TG113273.

THE EARLE ARMS is a traditional Norfolk village pub owned by the Heydon Hall estate. Built in the 16th century, the pub has remained relatively unchanged over the years and the bar is lit by candlelight in the

evenings. Open fires and a wood burner make this a very warm, welcoming pub in winter and the stone flagged floor is perfect for muddy paws. Food is available to eat in or take away and dog bowls are provided.
☎ 01263 587391.
⊕ www.theearlearms.com

Terrain: Quiet country roads, fields and woods characterise this walk. There are areas which can get very muddy depending on the weather and time of the year, so be prepared for a lot of mud! Almost all the walk is flat, but the surfaces can be very uneven.
Nearest vets: VAylsham Vets, 12 Hungate Street, Aylsham, NR11 6AA. ☎ 01263 732130.

The Walk

· ·

❶ Follow the gravel track in the corner of the village car park, passing eight trees planted in remembrance of the eight soldiers from Heydon who gave their lives during the First World War. Turn right on reaching the road, and walk away from the village along the quiet tree-lined country road. Livestock, including heritage sheep, can be seen in the surrounding fields. At the crossroads, cross over and walk straight ahead for about a mile along Salle Road with its grassy banks on either side, passing the sign to Field House Farm.

❷ Just after walking through a series of bends in the road, you will reach a wide opening in the hedge on the right with a gateway set back away from the road. (If you reach Stinton Hall Farm you've gone too far.) Take this turning and follow the wide grassy path straight ahead. The path leads between two long fields, with a ditch on one side. Livestock can be seen in the fields, including a bull so dogs must be kept on a lead. At the far end of the field, the path winds to the right, heading towards trees in the distance. Turn right on the path leading into the little wood.

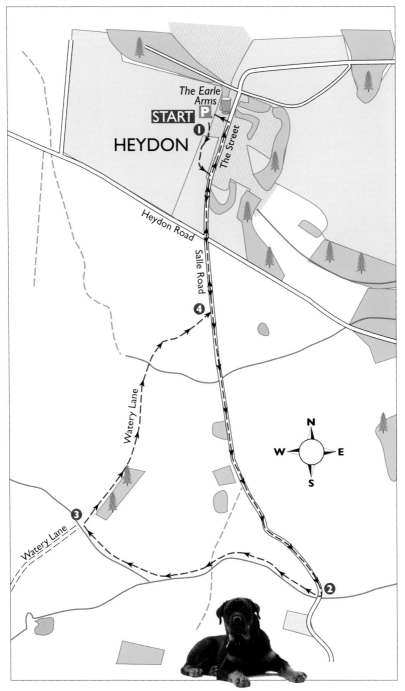

3 This path leads onto a wider track known locally as Watery Lane. Lined by deciduous trees on either side, the lane is used by farm vehicles. As the name suggests, the track can get very wet and muddy especially in the winter or after periods of heavy rain. A ditch appears part of the way along the track on the left-hand side. The vegetation on either side of the path changes along the route, to reveal more bracken, ivy and oaks, and the path becomes much firmer underfoot as you near the end of the lane.

4 In just over ½ mile you will reach Salle Road again, turn left and walk back to the crossroads, before retracing your steps to Heydon. Red kites can often be seeing flying overhead. If you want to extend the walk further beyond the pub, walk straight ahead past the church and into the grounds of Heydon Hall. Walkers are welcome to use the paths in the grounds on a permissive basis with dogs on leads at all times. There is no public right of way, and there is no access when livestock are in the parkland. The hard surface driveway leads up to the hall and round in a horseshoe style, covering roughly ½ mile.

12 CROMER CLIFFS
4½ miles (7.3 km)

Starting life as a fishing village, Cromer became a popular seaside resort attracting well-to-do tourists during the Victorian period. Much of its architecture reflects this development with lots of Victorian and Edwardian buildings, as well as a pier, and the long expanses of sand and pebble beaches continue to attract tourists today.

This walk takes you along the picturesque cliff-top to Overstrand and back via the beach. If the beach is impassable, there is a road option back to the start – just follow the signs to Cromer.

Note: Check the tide times if you wish to return via the beach as high tide can prevent access to the beach or leave you stranded. Details of tide times can be obtained online or at the RNLI Henry Blogg Museum near the Red Lion pub, close to the pier.

Start & Finish: Meadow Road Car Park.
Sat Nav: NR27 9DS.
Parking: Roads in Cromer get very busy, especially in the high season, making on-street parking difficult. The nearest public car park is Meadow Road Car Park located behind the North Norfolk Visitor Centre. This pay & display car park has both long and short stay parking facilities. There are toilets available in the Visitor Centre.
Map: OS Explorer 252 North Coast East. **Grid ref:** TG217420.

THE PUB THE RED LION, perched on top of East Cliff overlooking the pier, is a comfortable, popular pub attracting both tourists and locals. It serves local real ales within a bar and lounge area which still contains many original features. Homemade food is prepared fresh to order. Dogs are welcome in the bar and lounge, and have their own Doggy Bar, together with options of various doggy beverages including Pawsecco and Doggy Beer. Overnight accommodation is available, and even includes a dog bed. No parking on site.

☎ 01263 514964 ⊕ www.redlioncromer.co.uk

Terrain: Beach, town streets, promenade and cliff paths, some of which are steep and rough. The promenade does not go all the way to Overstrand but merges onto the beach, part of which is quite stony. Dogs can be let off the lead, but keep careful watch especially along the narrowest parts of the cliff-top path. During the high season, dogs may not be allowed on sections of the beach. Dogs and walkers are not allowed on the golf course. There are clear signs indicating the direction walkers should take. Depending on the time of year, it can get very muddy. No dog waste bins.

Nearest vets: Miramar Veterinary Centre, Old Station Yard, Norwich Road, Cromer, NR27 0HF. ☎ 01263 513976.

The Walk

● ●

❶ From the car park, cross over Louden Road in front of the North Norfolk Visitor Centre and walk straight ahead along Chapel Street. At the next road junction, turn right and walk down Church Street passing the church of St Peter & St Paul and Cromer Museum on your left, before taking the next left turning along Brook Street. Follow this road straight ahead to reach the Red Lion pub on your right-hand side.

❷ Follow the pathway round to the right, which is marked by black railings, and when you reach the road, cross over. There is a small park on your left, together with the RNLI Henry Blogg Museum containing details of tide times.

❸ Follow the path through the park, past the seating area and signed with an acorn. Keep walking straight ahead past the Henry Blogg Memorial Bust and bandstand, following the coast path towards Overstrand.

❹ In ¼ mile the path divides into two – the narrower route on the right is very steep, so take the left-hand path which widens out into a grassy area before rising steeply ahead. At the top of the rise, there is a seat with a path

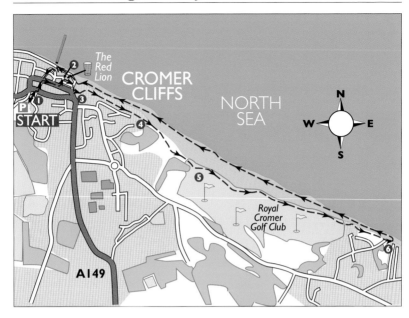

leading to the lighthouse on your right. Turn left, and continue to follow the path straight ahead. This section of the path is quite narrow in places, with thick vegetation on either side. It is uneven, with numerous variations in height. At intervals, there are good views of the beach far below.

5 When you reach the golf course, follow the signs to the left indicating the exact location of the path. Continue walking ahead along a much wider, flatter path. In around 1 mile the path leads past a group of houses.

6 To reach the beach, continue left. At the beach, turn left. Keep ahead for around 1 ½ miles until you reach the promenade leading into Cromer. Follow the path upwards past the museum and the Red Lion until you reach the pier. Turn left and head along Garden Street. At the junction, cross over and retrace your steps along Chapel Street to return to the car park.

If you are unable to return via the beach, either retrace your steps along the cliff top, or walk through Overstrand Beach Car Park (there are toilets here) and turn right at the road. Keep ahead and walk past the church. Look out for the amusing sign marked "on this site 7th September 1782 nothing happened". Turn onto the Cromer Road and continue walking for around 2 miles until you reach Cromer.

13 NEATISHEAD
3½ miles (5.6 km)

Dogs and their walkers will love this rural walk involving field paths and quiet roads, several of which are no-through roads. It skirts the edge of Barton Broad, the second largest of the Norfolk Broads, formed when medieval peat diggings were flooded due to the low water table. During the Second World War, RAF Neatishead became the first secret air defence radar centre. It is now home to the RAF Air Defence Radar Museum, tracing the history of the station, along with the Academy of Robotics headquarters.

Start & Finish: Barton Broad Main Car Park, Long Road.
Sat Nav: NR12 8XP.
Parking: Free parking is available at Barton Broad Main Car Park, where there are also some public toilets. Roadside parking is available outside the White Horse Inn.
Map: OS Explorer OL40 The Broads. **Grid ref:** TG351208.

THE PUB

THE WHITE HORSE INN, on The Street, is a real ale pub which brews its own beer on site and has a good selection of guest ales, lagers, ciders and other drinks. A glass panel in the bar allows you to take a look into the brewery while you are enjoying a drink. It offers a good selection of homemade food as well as a special pizza menu, which includes gluten free

options. Dogs are welcome in the bar area and the outside seating area. Staff will provide water for dogs on request.
☎ 01692 630828 ⊕ www.thewhitehorseinnneatishead.com

Terrain: The roads are very quiet, with little traffic. Dogs could be off lead when crossing fields. No stiles or dog waste bins. Note: Dogs are not allowed on the boardwalk leading through a conservation area to Neatishead Broad, guide dogs are the only exception.
Nearest vets: Westover Veterinary Centre, Hornbeam Road, North Walsham, NR28 0FX. ☎ 01692 403202.

The Walk

1 From Barton Broad car park, follow the gravel pathway to the left. The path widens out to include grassy areas alongside trees and brambles. On reaching the road, turn right. Go past the entrance to the Barton Broad Boardwalk (no dogs are allowed on the Boardwalk). Continue following the road straight ahead. The road winds to the right past houses named Herons Carr and Meadow Cottage.

2 At the crossroads, just past a postbox fixed to a

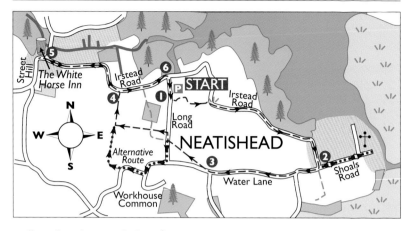

wall, walkers have a choice of routes.

A. Turn left for a short diversion towards the picturesque Irstead Church, which is approximately a five-minute walk. This is a no-through road and ends just past the church.

The church of St Michael in Irstead is a medieval flint church possessing a square tower and a roof thatched with local reed and sedge. St Michael's dragon is carved into a niche just above the door. If open, the church interior is well worth a look as it contains a beautiful screen painted with the figures of the Eleven Apostles and St John the Baptist, while the East Window was restored in memory of naturalist Sir Peter Scott, who is buried in the churchyard. Just past the church are Irstead Staithe and the River Ant.

B. Alternatively, turn right at the crossroads, and walk towards Workhouse Common. At the entrance to Old Hall on the left is an oak tree surrounded by iron fencing. The tree was planted to commemorate the coronation of Queen Elizabeth II. Continue straight ahead along Water Lane, passing a sign marked Broads by Bike No 8.

❸ In around ¾ mile look for a turning to the right leading to a footpath going diagonally across a field. Follow this track. At the road, turn right and take the next field path turning 20 metres ahead on your left. If agricultural work is underway and the field paths are impassable, turn left instead and follow the road until you reach the village of Workhouse Common. On the outskirts of the village, take the first turning to the right; follow the road straight ahead until a footpath appears on the right-hand side. This leads onto a wide grassy field path leading northwards towards the village of Neatishead.

If taking the field path route, keep straight ahead across the field. This leads onto a wide grassy path running between two fields. Turn right, and follow the path northwards until you reach the road.

4 At the end of the field path, turn left along Irstead Road until you reach the White Horse Inn.

5 On leaving the pub, retrace your steps past the Community shop (on your right-hand side). Follow the road through the village, passing the Neatishead Parish Council boat staithe on your left. A little further on is Grove Cottage where sometimes, during the summer, there is a wonderful stall outside selling homemade fudge from the Fudge Lady. Continue walking straight ahead.

6 In ¾ mile you'll reach Long Road where you turn right and the entrance to Barton Broad Main Car Park will be on your left.

14 THURNE
3 miles (5 km)

Thurne is a village within the Ludham & Potter Heigham Marshes. There are many water birds such as marsh harriers, herons, and waterfowl to be seen along the broad, and if you are lucky you may spot an otter. Windmills are also very much a feature of this walk, as several can be seen along the route. The walk offers a varied range of environments to interest any dog, and there are sections of the walk where dogs can run off lead with care.

> **Start & Finish:** The Lion, The Street, Thurne. **Sat Nav:** NR29 3AP.
> **Parking:** Park at the Lion if visiting, but please ask permission before leaving your car. Alternatively, park roadside in the village.
> **Map:** OS Explorer OL40 The Broads. **Grid ref:** TG403158.

THE PUB

THE LION is an award-winning village pub which attracts a lot of tourists during the summer season. A real ale pub, it also has an extensive gin menu. Both takeaway and eating in facilities are on offer and there is an attractive garden, bar and restaurant. Water bowls for thirsty dogs are available on request. Dogs are allowed in all the bar areas, but not in the main restaurant. Check website for opening times.

☎ 01692 671806 ⊕ www.thelionatthurne.com

Terrain: Permissive wide grassy footpaths, quiet roads, marshland and fields with firm flat paths providing good footing underneath. Although the route passes the river and staithes, the water is deep and dangerous so not suitable for dogs to swim in. Care also needs to be taken with regard to the presence of livestock and numerous water birds.

Nearest vets: Bridge Veterinary Practice, 63 Norwich Road, Wroxham, NR12 8RX. ☎ 01603 783920.

The Walk

1 With your back to the Lion inn, turn left and walk along the main village road past the staithe, postbox and red phone box. Keep ahead through the village until the road curves to the left. At this point turn right, keeping the thatched cottage on your right. Ahead is a sign for a permissive footpath. Go through the side gate, and walk down the wide grassy pathway with a hedge on one side, a fence on the other. Well behaved dogs could be let off the lead at this point, but take care dogs do not go into the fields on either side as livestock may be present. In the distance on the right, you can see the grey/black building of St Benet's drainage mill, as well as the White Mill of Thurne. Follow the path until you reach the staithe at the end, along which boats are moored.

2 Turn left. The water is deep here so do not let dogs swim. Ignore signs marked Wildlife Conservation

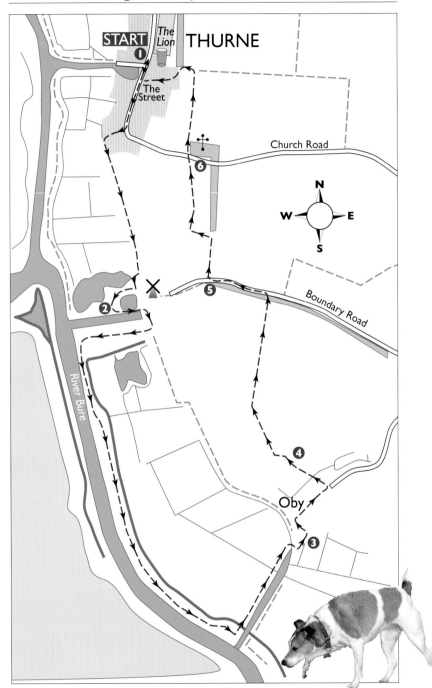

START
The Lion ❶
THURNE
The Street
Church Road
❻
N
W — E
S
❷
✕
❺
Boundary Road
River Bure
❹
Oby
❸

and Bureside Holiday Park, turn right and then sharp right again down the opposite side of the staithe. At the end of the staithe, turn left along the riverbank and walk along the Weavers' Way footpath for around a mile. In the distance the sail-less Upton Windmill, also known as Upton Black Mill, can be seen. Follow the path round to the left and then at the end of the staithe turn right.

3 Go through a gate which bears a sign marked 'Dogs to be kept on leads in this area' and turn left and then right to enter a long tree-lined path. The grassy path ends on a concrete road. Turn right and go through the squeeze gap, following the Weavers' Way sign on an old building. At the signposted junction turn left. This is a tree-lined public bridleway, and leads past farm buildings and through the farm but you should continue to follow the Weavers' Way signs. Livestock may be in the fields.

4 Follow the concrete path past an old shepherd hut on the left, behind the barn and left, around the edge of a field. The field path eventually turns to the right following the hedge line. There are extensive views across the meadows. Keep walking straight ahead between the fields following the hedge line round to the right. At the road turn left and head towards the campsite.

5 At the bend in the road, opposite the campsite, there is a gate on your right and a Weavers' Way sign. Take this footpath on your right, which follows the line of the hedge. Keep walking straight ahead until the end of the hedge. Turn left on the path, keeping the hedge on your left and field on your right. At the end of the field, the path winds to the right, leading towards a church in the distance. The hedge is now on your left.

6 Cross the road to the church. The church of St Edmund the Martyr is a thatched building, with an unusual flint chequerboard tower outlined in red. Follow the path to the left of the church, keeping the hedge on your left. Go through the kissing gate at the bottom of the field and follow the path past the farm. Horses are sometimes to be found in this field. Pass through the next kissing gate onto a concrete road. Turn left and follow the curving road through the farmyard and down to the staithe, passed at the beginning of the walk. At the road turn right to return to the pub and car park.

15 WINTERTON-ON-SEA

3 or 4 miles (5 or 6.4 km)

Winterton-on-Sea is a pretty seaside village with a beautiful unspoilt beach stretching for miles in either direction, providing lots of space for dogs to run and paddle in the sea. Dog walkers are recommended to stay on the area south of Winterton, as walking northwards can cause problems with the extensive seal populations which breed on the beach.

The combination of sandy beach, sea, flat paths and undulating dunes give this route plenty of interest for both dogs and their owners. In winter, the Norfolk Coast Path route offers some shelter from the east winds, but care does have to be taken on the beach as waves can be strong, and there are continual risks of erosion among the dunes.

> **Start & Finish:** Fishermans Return, The Lane, Winterton-on-Sea.
> **Sat Nav:** NR29 4BN.
> **Parking:** Park at Fishermans Return if visiting, but please ask permission before leaving your car. Alternatively, there is roadside parking just by the pub on The Lane or park at Winterton Beach Car Park and start the walk from point 2.
> **Map:** OS Explorer OL40 The Broads. **Grid ref:** TG495194.

THE PUB **FISHERMANS RETURN** is a 300-year-old brick and flint pub located within the coastal village of Winterton-on-Sea. A large pub, it also provides accommodation. A new extension at the back offers extra seating, function rooms, live music and a private beer garden. Specials change regularly, reflecting availability of local produce and all fish is sourced daily from Lowestoft, with meat and game from local butchers. Light bites such as jacket potatoes and sandwiches are available until 5pm. The pub is very dog friendly and water-filled dog bowls are readily available.

☎ 01493 393305 ⊕ www.fishermansreturn.com

Terrain: A mixture of firm and soft terrain with sandy beach, dunes, grassland varying from flat to undulating. Two dog waste bins are located along the Norfolk Coast Path.

Nearest vets: Caister Vets, 5 Ormesby Road, Caister-on-Sea, NR30 5JY. ☎ 01493 809766.

The Walk

1 On leaving the pub car park, turn left into The Lane. At the junction, turn left again opposite The Hallway and walk down King Street. This is a quiet residential road, and there is no footpath. On reaching the village hall, turn right into Beach Road and keep going until you come to the beach car park. This is an area vulnerable to erosion during storms and access points to the beach may change.

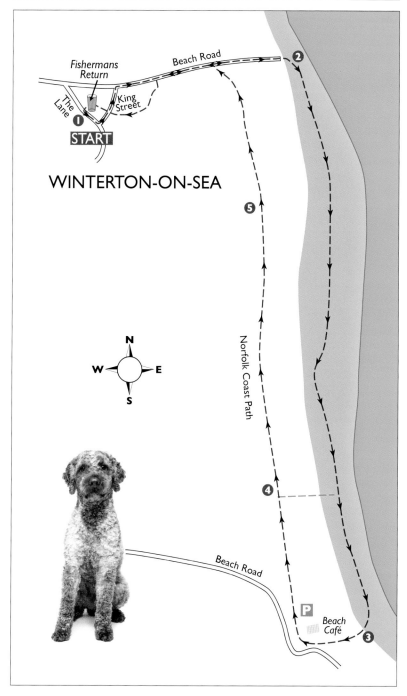

Fishermans Return

Beach Road

The Lane

King Street

START

WINTERTON-ON-SEA

N
W E
S

Norfolk Coast Path

Beach Road

P

Beach Café

2 Walk through the car park and follow the gap through the dunes to the beach. Turn right and continue walking ahead for around two miles until you reach Hemsby Gap. (Dogs are not allowed on the Hemsby Beach Gap between Easter to October. The alternative route is to turn right 500 metres before the gap, and walk up the wide sandy footpath and turn right, and then follow directions from point 4.) The North Sea tides can come in quite fast, and reach the dunes especially during very high tides. At Hemsby Gap you'll see a structure on the beach which is easily identifiable by its V-shaped concrete blocks, and once served as a pillbox guarding the beach during the Second World War. Turn right and walk up the beach towards a wooden signpost which heralds the entrance to the Gap.

3 Leaving the beach, walk up the path towards the local beachside shops. Turn right by the signpost indicating the route of the Norfolk Coast Path, heading through the car park and past Stonehenge Crazy Golf. Keep ahead through the next car park. Adders have been seen in this area and dog walkers should keep watch for them. The car park ends in an extensive, wide stretch of open grass with a narrow gateway at the far end, marked by a post with a yellow arrow and an acorn symbol. The narrow path leads downhill between bracken, gorse and grass. The path soon widens to become much firmer grass

and sand underfoot. Dogs can be let off lead here as it is ideal for a good run. The central path is quite wide, edged by tall dunes on the right and bracken rising steeply upwards towards a row of houses on the left.

4 At a crossing point, giving access to the houses on the left, and the beach on the right, you'll find a dog waste bin. Cross over the path and continue walking ahead. This is where you will have rejoined the walk if you have taken the shorter route. Another dog waste bin is located about 100 metres further on. This also marks the start of a section of the Norfolk Coast Path and an area containing unusual acidic soils, rare plants and animals such as natterjack toads, breeding and over-wintering birds, dragonflies, fragile areas of mosses, lichens, heather and dune grass. Walkers are requested to stay on the paths and keep dogs under close supervision in this area. The terrain now becomes very undulating, with a wide central path, plus smaller paths leading off through areas of bracken and grassland. All the paths meander slightly, and can be steep in places. Keep walking ahead. The lighthouse and church tower at Winterton-on-Sea can be seen in the distance ahead and an area of native woodland appears on the left containing oak and beech trees. The path can vary between being firm and very soft sand, winding to one side or the other of large holes with sand at the bottom – perfect for dogs to roll in!

5 Approaching Winterton-on-Sea, look to the left to see the unusual, colourful round houses. *The Hermanus roundhouses, visible from the Norfolk Coast path, are an unusual sight. The colourful yellow, pink, blue and mint green African-style roundhouses complete with conical thatched roofs were inspired by the rondavels of Hermanus Bay in South Africa. A previous owner of the site had spent time living in South Africa and built these houses in memory.*

The path leads past a roped-off area on the right, and becomes much softer underfoot. Keep walking ahead until you reach Beach Road from the beginning of the walk. Turn left along the pavement and head back into Winterton. The church tower can be seen directly ahead. Turn left into King's Corner, beside the Church Rooms, an area named after a local man, Ivan King 1903-1972. Follow the road ahead, past the pretty village hall garden until you reach the back entrance of the Fishermans Return pub on the right.

16 HETHERSETT
3¼ or 4 miles (5.2 or 6.5 km)

Hethersett is a large village with a long history. In 1549, participants in Kett's Rebellion met under an oak tree on the road between Wymondham and Hethersett before marching on Norwich. Kett's Oak can still be seen beside the B1172 near Hethersett. The area covered by the walk lies between the B1172 and the A11, passing through arable farmland and along traditional paths edged by woodland well known for its wildlife. The route can get very muddy in places, and varies from pavements to rough field tracks. In spring and early summer the field path wild flowers bloom in the uncultivated field edges.

> **Start & Finish:** The Kings Head, 36 Norwich Road, Hethersett.
> **Sat Nav:** NR9 3DD.
> **Parking:** Park at the Kings Head if visiting, but please ask permission before leaving your car. Alternatively, there is some roadside parking right outside the pub.
> **Map:** OS Explorer 237 Norwich – Wymondham, Attleborough & Watton. **Grid ref:** TG154045.

THE PUB

THE KINGS HEAD is a large traditional pub, dating back to the 17th century. The pub garden is linked to a community-based project, Nature's Neighbours, designed to protect existing wildlife and encourage biodiversity. As a result, the garden includes a pond, bird houses, a hedgehog house and squirrel post together with over 15 native trees. There

> **Terrain:** Mainly flat terrain along pavements, field edges, tracks, paths and woodland. There is a dog waste bin beside the Priory gateway close to the start of the walk.
> **Nearest vets:** Rowan House Vets, 28 Queen's Road, Hethersett, NR9 3DB. ☎ 01953 600066.

is also an area dedicated to growing produce for the pub. The lunch menu includes smaller plates and sandwiches along with a good range of traditional choices. Dogs are welcome both inside and outside in the garden. Dog bowls and water are provided. ☎ 01603 813411 ⊕ www.kingshethersett.co.uk

The Walk

1 With your back to the pub, turn right and walk along Norwich Road until you reach the B1172, passing a dog waste bin beside the Priory gateway. Turn right and follow the pavement alongside the B1172. This is a moderately busy local road leading to Wymondham. Keep ahead past Old Hall police training centre on your left and cross the road at the next crossing, just past the training centre exit. Turn right and keep walking along the wide grassy verge for 200 metres until you reach a field gate on your left-hand side, just before a bus shelter.

2 Entering the field, follow the permissive path to the right keeping parallel with the road. Keep walking along the field edge as it winds to the left around a building, then back towards the hedge bordering the road. When a no entry sign appears to the left, keep walking directly ahead and go through the narrow gap in the hedge. Cross the driveway leading to Park Farm Hotel, aiming for the gap in the hedge on the far side. The path continues straight ahead, following the line of the hedge before winding left past the back of a cottage. At the telegraph pole, turn right and follow the field edge to continue walking parallel with the road.

3 Turn left at the corner of the field, and follow the path along the field edge. There are ditches on the right-hand side hidden by undergrowth. Keep walking ahead until you reach a no entry sign, and a field entrance to the

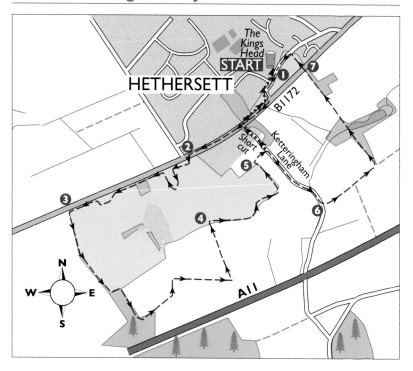

right. Pass through the field entrance keeping the small wood on your right-hand side and follow the path as it winds to the left and then right and then left again.

4 Go through the gap into the next field, following the field path round to the right towards a farm building with a very decorative black and red tiled roof, marked with large Xs. Keeping the farm building on your right continue to follow the field edge round to the right and then left until you reach a gap in the hedge on the far side. A small pond can be seen on the right.

5 Go through the gap leading onto a playing field and turn right towards a gate. You are now on a small local road, Ketteringham Lane. For the shorter walk turn left and when the lane reaches the B1172, cross over and turn right to retrace your steps back along Norwich Road to the Kings Head. For a longer walk, turn right along Ketteringham Lane. There is no footpath, but there are rough verges beside the hedges. When the hedges open out into fields on either side, look for a footpath sign on the left-hand side.

6 Turn left onto the track where you will see a hedge directly in front dividing two fields. Follow the wider track to the right-hand side of the hedge. This quiet lane, known as Suckling Lane, is sometimes used by farm vehicles and there are deep ruts in the pathway. In 400m you'll come to a wood where there is a rusty, partly hidden metal gate on the left, beside a footpath marker. Turn left through the gate and between the trees, taking the route known as Kissing Alley. In winter or after heavy rain, this part of the path can get very muddy. A very shady path, it passes through native woodland and there are lots of birds to be heard.

7 The path emerges onto the B1172, beside a public footpath marker. Cross the road, aiming for the big wooden gates directly opposite. To the left of the gates is a footpath marker, which you follow to continue along Kissing Alley. Cross Norwich Road at the end of the path, and turn left. Keep ahead along the pavement until you reach the Kings Head on your right.

17 CHEDGRAVE
2½ miles (3.8 km)

A pretty combination of edge-of-town, river and open countryside, this area creates an interesting and varied walk. The village of Chedgrave is located on the Wherryman's Way long-distance footpath linking Norwich and Great Yarmouth and is one of the less frequently visited Broads. The route passes through reed beds, along the River Chet as well as through Chedgrave Common, a County Wildlife Site. If you are lucky, you may see herons, woodpeckers, kingfishers, marsh harriers and otters during the walk.

Start & Finish: Loddon Staithe Car Park, Bridge Street, Chedgrave.
Sat Nav: NR14 6EZ.
Parking: Park at the Loddon Staithe Public Conveniences Car Park, just off Bridge Street.
Map: OS Explorer OL40 The Broads. **Grid ref:** TM361989.

THE PUB THE WHITE HORSE is a friendly village pub, with a large garden. Open daily the pub offers a good range of real ales and gins, freshly ground coffee and hot chocolate along with a range of hot meals. Dogs are welcome in the bar and garden where water and biscuits are available.
☎ 01508 520250 ⊕ www.whitehorsechedgrave.co.uk

> **Terrain:** Mostly flat, using pavements, tracks and riverbank paths, there are areas which can get very muddy after heavy rain. For much of the way, dogs are best kept on leads due to the presence of wildlife. There is a bin for dog waste on Hardley Road.
> **Nearest vets:** Three Rivers Veterinary Group, 19 Beccles Road, Loddon, NR14 6JQ. ☎ 01508 520247.

The Walk

1 On leaving the car park turn right along Bridge Street. If visiting the White Horse follow the road round to the left and the pub is on your left. To continue the walk, keep ahead on the bend to walk up Langley Road. At the crossroads turn right into Hardley Road. Follow the road until you reach a side turning towards the church of All Saints with its pretty lychgate. Instead of heading directly towards the church, keep left on the grass to cross a small green known as The Pits and a children's play area. Dogs must be on a lead.

2 At the far side of the playground turn right onto Pits Lane, following the red sign for Wherryman's Way. There are no pavements but this is a quiet road providing vehicular access to the staithe. Dogs must still be kept on a lead. As the road winds sharply right, aim for the gateway straight ahead marked with a signpost for the Wherryman's Way. This path has a hard surface, is accessible all year round and leads to Chedgrave Staithe and the River Chet. There are views towards a church in the distance. The long straight path passes open countryside and a wood with large willow trees. The river and staithe are navigable, and are used extensively by boats cruising around the Southern Broads. The water is deep, and there are free moorings on the opposite side of the river while on the other side of the path there is a deep ditch. Look out for wildlife in this area, with herons and marsh harriers being frequent visitors.

3 *At the far end of the path, a section of the mast from Hathor is on display. Hathor is a pleasure wherry built in 1905 by Hall of Reedham for the Colman family and is now owned by the Wherry Yacht Charter Charitable Trust. A wherry is a type of sail boat used extensively on the Broads transporting goods and people.* The path diverges at this point, away from the Wherryman's Way route. For a longer walk you

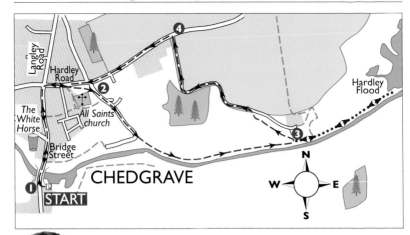

can keep ahead along a narrower path leading down a spur to Hardley Flood, an area of lagoons and reed beds and a biological Site of Special Scientific Interest. This path is much rougher, and after periods of heavy rain, can flood. There are boardwalks taking the path over creeks and the final boardwalk offers a superb view of Hardley Flood. You will then need to retrace your steps back to the Hathor mast. To continue the main route, pass through the gate located

beside the Hathor mast, following the signs for the Wherryman's Way. This path goes across a field towards some houses. Before reaching the houses, turn left across the unmarked Chedgrave Common on a grass path. In the far corner there is a small gate giving access to the road where you turn left. This is an unmade and potholed road, with fences and brambles on either side known as the Common Loke. Follow this road until you reach a T-junction.

4 Here there is a bin for dog waste beside the signpost marking the Wherryman's Way. Turn left onto Hardley Road, heading back into the village of Chedgrave. There is no footpath at this point so use the field verges to allow for passing traffic. Keep ahead along this road, passing All Saints Church, seen earlier in the walk. At the crossroads turn left down Langley Road, retracing your steps back to the car. If visiting the pub turn right along Norwich Road and the White Horse can be seen just across the road on the left.

18 THE PULHAMS
3 miles (5 km)

Set in rural South Norfolk, surrounded by farmland, The Pulhams comprise two villages – Pulham Market and Pulham St Mary, of which Pulham Market is the larger. Often described as one of the prettiest villages in South Norfolk, Pulham Market has a large village green surrounded by numerous thatched cottages and a medieval church. Pulham St Mary is also a busy village, with its own medieval church and was originally the site of the Royal Navy Air Service Airship Station, which later became RAF Pulham from 1918 to 1958. The area is dotted with buildings once used on the airfield. This is an easy to follow route through open countryside, fields, quiet lanes and along a well-maintained pavement between the two villages. Dogs can be let off-lead while walking through the fields.

Start & Finish: The Crown Inn, Harleston Road, Pulham Market.
Sat Nav: IP21 4TA.
Parking: Park at the Crown Inn if visiting, but please ask permission before leaving your car. Alternatively, there is roadside parking opposite and to the right of the pub on Station Road.
Map: OS Explorer 230 Diss & Harleston. **Grid ref:** TM197861.

THE PUB | **THE CROWN INN** is a 15th-century country inn which is owned and run by the local community. Inside, an open fireplace offers warmth in winter, and an array of comfortable chairs make it a good place to relax after a walk. Dogs are very welcome here and have their own doggy menu with delicacies including pigs' ears and a doggy roast. The only area where dogs are not allowed is the Reading Room, which is a dog free dining area.

☎ 01379 831239 ⊕ www.thecrowninnpulham.co.uk

Alternatively, try **THE FALCON**, a small, dog-friendly community pub located on The Green. ☎ 01379 763234 ⊕ www.thefalconpulham.co.uk

---

Terrain: Field paths, local lanes and a local road with pavement. There are dog bins in Station Road near the start of the walk, just before Dirty Lane, and another on leaving Pulham St Mary.
Nearest vets: : Cherry Tree Vets, 3 Broad Street, Harleston, IP20 9AZ.
☎ 01379 852999.

The Walk

1 Turn left out of the pub, and walk down Station Road where you will get a good view of the large stone church. There is a pavement part of the way, before it enters open countryside. In ¼ mile, turn left by the public footpath sign, opposite Walnut Cottage. A dog bin can be found at this point. The path is firm underfoot, and broad in places as it winds through a small wooded area of mainly deciduous trees. The path winds to the right and crosses a small wooden bridge across a stream. Take care as there are no handholds. Turn left and walk along the wide track next to the field edge, following the lines of telegraph wires. Go through the hedge at the end of the field, crossing over a metal grid bridge. Continue walking straight ahead along the edge of this long cultivated field, with a deep stream on the left, bordered by nettles and brambles.

2 At the end of the field, you will reach a concrete and steel Bailey bridge, used mainly as a storage, maintenance and salvage yard. Turn right away from the bridge, and walk straight ahead past an extensive hardstanding. Ignore signs for a footpath beside a stile on the left as this leads into a field where there are usually cattle and bulls. Instead, take the left-hand turning just beyond the tree line. This is a wide, firm, flat track which was formerly part of the Beccles to Tivetshall railway line (Waveney Valley Line) which closed in 1966. Walk on along the track following the line of telegraph wires. This is a well used, popular dog walking route passing through open fields with tall hedges on the right.

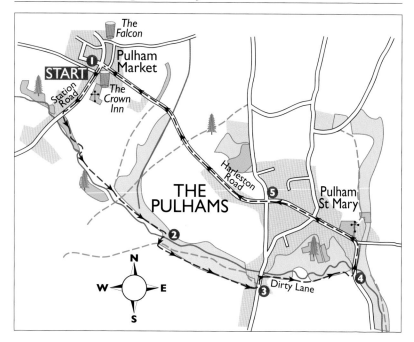

3 The long straight track eventually passes another area of hardstanding on the right-hand side, before reaching a T-junction where you turn left. There is no footpath at this point but this is a quiet road, used mainly by local vehicles. There is a dog waste bin a little further along the road on the left. Turn right into Dirty Lane, a narrow country lane with a hard tarmac surface. Little used by cars, it is lined by tall hedges and trees and is popular with dog walkers. As the road begins to curve to the right, a dog bin can be found on the left-hand side.

4 At the end of the lane and 'Give Way' sign, turn left into Harleston Road and cross the little bridge. Take care because this is the main road between Pulham Market and Harleston and can be quite busy. A pavement appears on the left-hand side soon after crossing the bridge. Keep ahead as the road curves to the left, past a signpost on the far side. The route now leads through the village of Pulham St Mary, passing the village church. *Although there has been a church on this site since Anglo Saxon times, the existing church of St Mary the Virgin dates back to the mid-13th century and has a square tower containing 8 bells. It has several rare, early English sculptural elements and an impressive porch decorated with angels and an ornate pierced parapet. Continue along the road past the village sign. Pulham St Mary was once a major site for military airships and on either side of the sign are the images of the R33 and R34 airships*

along with a commemorative plaque underneath *telling their story.* Crossing over Station Road, keep ahead past the Pennoyer Centre. Built in Victorian times as the village school, it was eventually closed in the late 20th century and later renovated as part of a community led project. It now acts as a community centre and has a café providing food and drink.

5 The route is now a straight road for ¾ mile leading to Pulham Market. It passes rows of houses and an allotment before reaching the countryside. There is a dog waste bin available just after exiting the village. The pavement is quite wide, flat and firm and the road is moderately busy, mainly with local vehicles passing between the A140 and Harleston. On entering the village of Pulham Market, the path narrows alongside a tall wall just past the village school but then widens out as you reach the large village green. The Crown Inn can be seen on your left-hand side, just past the church and The Falcon is to your right just across the green.

19 FRENZE BECK NATURE RESERVE
2½ miles (4.2 km)

Frenze Beck Nature Reserve was developed in 2003 from grazing marshland and is now a wetland and meadow wildlife haven. Surprisingly quiet and peaceful despite the nearness of the business park and main roads, this is a walk which can be shortened or lengthened depending on the number of side paths you choose to take. Mostly flat terrain, the main path leads past extensive reed beds, along a river, through meadows and wild flower areas offering constantly changing scenic beauty. Among the wildlife that may be seen along the way are pipistrelle bats, squirrels, birds of prey and rabbits. Woodpeckers may also be heard among the trees. Yellow flag irises provide splashes of colour in season, as do the bright red berries of the rowan trees and the vast array of wild flowers in the meadows. There are seats at intervals mainly along the riverside area offering a pleasant spot to relax.

> **Start & Finish:** Frenze Beck Nature Reserve Car Park, Sawmills Road, Diss. **Sat Nav:** IP22 4GG.
> **Parking:** Park at Frenze Beck Nature Reserve car park. There is also some alternative parking adjacent to the Ampersand Brew Co.
> **Map:** OS Explorer 230 Diss & Harleston. **Grid ref:** TM131793.

THE PUB
THE AMPERSAND BREW TAP is part brewery, part shop and part bar. It is a family-owned local brewer, offering a varying range of beers, cider, wine and other drinks and snacks. The main brewing takes place on a different site, but this is where the beer is finished, ready to drink. Opening hours vary by season. The shop is open in the daytime while the Brewery Tap is open at weekends and evenings, and frequently from late afternoon during the week. The food on offer is equally varied ranging from curries to pizzas, supplied by takeaway vans selling local produce mainly in the late

> **Terrain:** Mainly flat terrain, some slopes, woodland & field paths. Some road walking.
> **Nearest vets:** Linden House Veterinary Centre, 70 Mission Road, Diss, IP22 4HX. ☎ 01379 651183.

afternoons/evenings. There is a large outdoor seating area, as well as indoor facilities. Dogs are welcome in the outside seating area.
☎ 01379 643944 ⊕ www.ampersandbrew.co

The Walk

. . . .

① From the car park at Frenze Beck follow the broad grassy path leading onto the reserve. Turn right at the signboard along a firm, bark path which

leads through the trees, before winding to the left down a slope, edged by a wooden fence. Large expanses of reed beds can be seen on the left, with patches of nettles and tall grass on the right. Views of Frenze Beck appear and disappear as you walk along the path. It is not a good idea to allow dogs to try the water, as it is very green and there are lots of algae. Passing a wooden bench and lifebuoy near the beck, the path continues past a series of what look like dead hedges in front of the reed bed area. These hedges are actually pruned tree branches, which are laid horizontally and allowed to decompose, creating a home for wildlife.

② Ignore the path on the left (unless you want a shortcut back to your car) and continue walking straight ahead along the main path following the line of the river. Another seat and lifebuoy can be seen on the left, as well as several small paths which circle round to rejoin the main path. Cross the little bridge, marked by wooden fences on either side, (although it is hard to see any difference in the undergrowth surrounding it). The beck becomes almost hidden behind large expanses of nettles on the right-hand side and views of the business park appear in the distance as the path opens up into a wide rough meadow. Winding to the left, the path crosses an extensive grassy area with sections of tall grass and wild flowers. Turn right at the next bench and follow the path as it winds to the left towards the edge of the reserve, adjacent to the business park buildings. Do not take the side path heading across boards as it leads to a field inhabited by cattle, with locked gates.

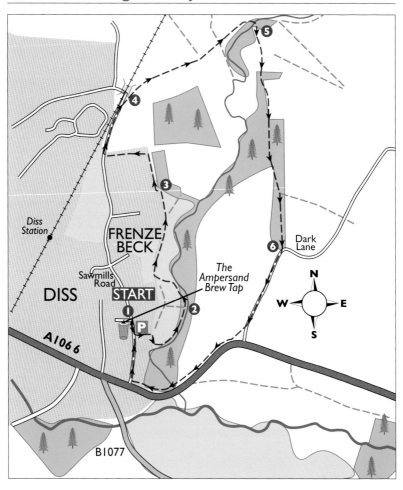

3 Keeping the business park buildings directly on your left, follow the path to the left of the trees. At the picnic bench, turn left and walk ahead until you reach a gate with a dog bin just outside. This leads onto a busy, narrow road with no footpath so take care. Turn right, keeping to the right against the traffic and walk ahead until you reach some traffic lights.

4 Just before the railway bridge take the turning onto a track on the right-hand side with a dog bin at the entrance. Continue on the track around a vehicle gate and between fields usually occupied by cattle. At the ford, dogs can be allowed to paddle in the water but bear in mind it does get deep in places as this is quite a fast river. Do not attempt to cross the ford. To cross the river follow the narrow fenced path to the left, which leads beside the river,

and soon reaches a narrow wooden bridge leading into a wood. Follow the sloping rough path between the trees.

5 The path emerges onto a field track beside a signpost marked Angles Way/Boudicca Way. Turn right then sharp left and follow the track past St Andrew's Church on your left. *This is now in the care of the Churches Conservation Trust and is usually open to visitors. Dating back to 1294, this small church contains a quite spectacular square carved box pew near the altar, along with two ornate carved chairs. Further along the track you'll see a number of hangars and sheds. These were used by USAAF Thorpe Abbotts and the 100th Bomb Group to house B-17s in the Second World War.* Follow the track past the stone walls of Frenze Hall and keep ahead through trees on either side. This track is narrow and used by cars and agricultural vehicles, with bordering fields usually containing grazing cattle so take care and keep dogs on leads.

6 At the end of the concrete track turn right. Follow this country road for around 400 metres and just before the road meets a busy main road, look for a grassy field path on the right. If closed, keep ahead to the main road and turn right along the footpath. If open, follow this long flat permissive path until you reach an opening in the hedge on the left-hand side. Dogs must be kept on leads. Turn left onto the footpath, then turn right and walk ahead on the pavement against the traffic. At the traffic lights, turn right past the car showroom and walk along the pavement to return to the car park. The Ampersand Brew Tap can be seen on the left-hand side of the road just after the entrance to Frenze Beck.

20 GARBOLDISHAM
1½ miles (2.6 km)

Garboldisham is a Breckland village on the border of South Norfolk and Suffolk, and is bisected by the A1066. This route takes in the northern side of the village, all of which is in Norfolk and, being an agricultural area, it includes several water meadows grazed by cows. This is a pleasant, short relaxing walk through open countryside, water marshes and woods. It is fairly flat, although there is one area involving steep steps to walk down. Most of the paths are wide, and it is possible to let dogs off leads for much of the route.

Start & Finish: The Fox Inn, The Street. **Sat Nav:** IP22 2RZ.
Parking: Some parking at the side of the Fox Inn, plus an upper car park accessed from the A1066.
Map: OS Explorer 230 Diss & Harleston. **Grid ref:** TM006815.

THE PUB

THE FOX INN, located at the junction of the A1066 and B1111, is a Grade II listed building dating back to the 17th century. It has been a community-owned pub since 2016 and volunteers have undertaken a major restoration, revealing original brickwork and timbers. Dogs are welcome and water bowls are provided in the garden. Open weekends and some weekdays but check the website for opening times.
☎ 01953 688538 ⊕ www.garboldishamfox.co.uk

> **Terrain:** Field paths, woodland, pavements and one flight of steps. There are places where dogs can be safely let off the lead for a run but leads are essential along the path by the water meadow as cows graze in the adjacent fields. A dog waste bin is located halfway up Back Street.
>
> **Nearest vets:** Linden House Veterinary Centre, 70 Mission Road, Diss, IP22 4HX. ☎ 01379 651183. Uplands Way Vets Ltd, Low Road, Bressingham, Diss, IP22 2AA. ☎ 01379 642865.

The Walk

1 Cross the B1111 in front of the pub, towards the War Memorial, and head down Church Road opposite. You will pass Garboldisham Village Hall on the right-hand side and then St John the Baptist Church on the left. At the end of Church Road, ignore the right-hand turning into Back Street, and follow the road winding to your left out of the village.

2 Just before the end of the road, there is a signed public footpath on your right-hand side, pointing towards a wide grassy path between two open fields. Turn right along the footpath and walk straight ahead.

3 In ¼ mile you will reach a metal gate on your left. Go through the gate, and keep walking ahead along the path. At the far end of the wood, turn right and follow the field path to the next field entrance. Turn right and continue walking straight ahead.

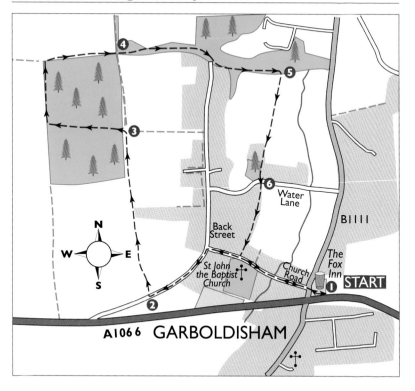

4 At the end of the pathway, there is a public footpath sign. Continue walking straight ahead. This is a narrower path passing through a small area of deciduous woodland. It leads out onto a field edge, with more deciduous trees and a ditch on the right-hand side and a fence on the left. At the end of the path, ignore the exit to the right facing a thatched house leading onto Back Street. Instead, follow the left-hand path to continue winding through the trees. Eventually the path widens out, becoming mixed woodland. There is a long brick estate wall on the left-hand side, and at one point you pass an arched gateway complete with an iron gate.

5 At the bottom of the woodland path, turn right following the tree-lined pathway through the water meadows in which cows often graze. The path is wide and well trodden, offering views across the meadows on either side with more thatched cottages to be seen in the distance on the right-hand side. Walk through the dual gates, carefully arranged to allow cows to be moved from one meadow to the other. The second gate leads onto a gravelled drive in front of a yellow painted house, complete with plaster pargeting in the form of Tudor roses. There is public access across the driveway. Keep ahead, through the gate at the far side which leads to a tree-lined driveway heading down to Water Lane.

6 At the junction with Water Lane, pause for a minute to see the ruined church tower on the right. *This is all that remains of All Saints church, which was built in 1305 for the use of villagers, unlike St John the Baptist church which was built by the Lord of the Manor. The two churches operated separately until 1450, when they were amalgamated. During the succeeding centuries, All Saints gradually fell into disuse and in 1734, the villagers obtained permission from the Bishop of Norwich to allow the church to fall down. The tombs were moved to St John's and the church building decayed with stone being taken for use elsewhere in the village. Now all that remains is part of the stone tower, and an area maintained by the villagers as a wild flower area.*

Cross over Water Lane at the footpath sign and follow the pathway ahead. This narrow country path runs between hedging and farmland. On the left-hand side, the B1111 can be seen in the distance. It is believed that the Old Rectory was in this area, so the pathway would have been used by the priest and his family to reach the church. The path ends in a flight of steps emerging directly opposite the entrance to the church of St John the Baptist. Turn left and retrace your steps back to the Fox Inn.

A SELECTION OF OTHER DOG FRIENDLY COUNTRY PUBS IN NORFOLK

ACLE – Acle Bridge Inn
ASHILL – The White Hart
AYLSHAM – The Porters Arms
BANNINGHAM – The Banningham Crown
BINHAM – The Chequers Inn
BLAKENEY – The White Horse
BLICKLING – The Bucks Arms
BRAMERTON – The Water's Edge
BURNHAM MARKET – The Hoste
CLEY-NEXT-THE-SEA – The George & Dragon
COLTISHALL – The Rising Sun
CROMER – The Kings Head, The Wellington (The Welly)
DEREHAM – The Cock
FAKENHAM – The Crown, Running Horse
FRITTON – The Fritton Arms
GREAT YARMOUTH – The Kings Arms
HEACHAM – The West Norfolk, Bushel & Strike
HEMSBY – The Lacon Arms

HOLME – The White Horse
HOLT – The Kings Head
HORNING – The Swan Inn
HOVETON – Kings Head Hotel
HUNSTANTON – The Mariner
LANGHAM – The Blue Bell
LODDON – The Swan
LUDHAM – King's Arms
MORSTON – The Anchor Inn
NORTH WALSHAM – The Peasants' Tavern
OXBOROUGH – Bedingfeld Arms
REEPHAM – The Kings Arms
SALTHOUSE – The Dun Cow
SCOLE – Crossways Inn
SHERINGHAM – The Two Lifeboats, The Robin Hood
SNETTISHAM – Rose & Crown
STANHOE – The Duck
STOKESBY – The Ferry Inn
SWAFFHAM – The White Hart
TASBURGH – The Countryman
WEYBOURNE – The Maltings